INTIMACY IN LATER LIFE

INTIMACY IN LATER LIFE

KATE DAVIDSON & GRAHAM FENNELL
EDITORS

Transaction Publishers
New Brunswick (U.S.A.) and London (U.K.)

Second printing 2009
Copyright © 2004 by Transaction Publishers, New Brunswick, New Jersey. Chapters 1, 3, 4, 5, 6, and 8 were originally published in Ageing International, Fall 2002, Vol. 27, No. 4 and Chapter 2 in Winter 2001-2002, Vol. 27, No. 1.

All rights reserved under International and Pan-American Copyright Conventions. No part of this book may be reproduced or transmitted in any form or by any means, electronic or mechanical, including photocopy, recording, or any information storage and retrieval system, without prior permission in writing from the publisher. All inquiries should be addressed to Transaction Publishers, Rutgers—The State University, 35 Berrue Circle, Piscataway, New Jersey 08854-8042.

This book is printed on acid-free paper that meets the American National Standard for Permanence of Paper for Printed Library Materials.

Library of Congress Catalog Number: 2004046058
ISBN: 978-0-7658-0557-7
Printed in the United States of America

Library of Congress Cataloging-in-Publication Data

Intimacy in later life / Kate Davidson and Graham Fennell, editors.
    p. cm.
Includes bibliographical references and index.
ISBN 0-7658-0557-X (alk. paper)
    1. Aged—Psychology. 2. Interpersonal relations. 3. Aged—Sexual behavior. I. Davidson, Kate, 1947- II. Fennell, Graham.

HQ1061.I555 2004
306.7'084'6—dc22   2004046058

Contents

Introduction: New Intimate Relationships in Later Life *Kate Davidson and Graham Fennell*	vii
1. Intimacy and Autonomy, Gender and Ageing: Living Apart Together *Sofie Ghazanfareeon Karlsson and Klas Borell*	1
2. Late-Life Widowhood in the United States: New Directions in Research and Theory *Deborah Carr and Rebecca Utz*	19
3. Re-Engaging: New Partnerships in Late-Life Widowhood *Nan Stevens*	47
4. Gender Differences in New Partnership Choices and Constraints for Older Widows and Widowers *Kate Davidson*	65
5. The Dilemma of Repartnering: Considerations of Older Men and Women Entering New Intimate Relationships in Later Life *Jenny de Jong Gierveld*	85
6. Attitudes of Older Widows and Widowers in New Brunswick, Canada Towards New Partnerships *Deborah Kestin van den Hoonaard*	105
7. The "Current Woman" in an Older Widower's Life *Alinde J. Moore and Dorothy C. Stratton*	121
8. Perceptions of Remarriage by Widowed People in Singapore *Kalyani K. Mehta*	143
Contributors	161
Index	163

Introduction: New Intimate Relationships in Later Life

Kate Davidson and Graham Fennell

To love and be loved is arguably one of the most powerful and fundamental driving forces for sustaining self-esteem and self-identity throughout the life course. For partners in a romantic relationship, this love is commonly expressed through sexual intimacy. The need for reciprocal loving does not change as we grow older, however, what can change are the circumstances in which we are able to maintain previous levels of sexual activity. For example, poor health of self or partner can reduce the ability or indeed the desire for sexual intercourse, but does not necessarily preclude a degree of physical intimacy within a continuing loving relationship. A partner may undergo personality change and become a different person from the partner with whom we fell in love, for instance through the long-term effects of alcohol damage, stroke, or dementia. Rather more dramatic is the loss of a partner, which in later life is the most common reason for cessation of sexual activity. We know relatively little about the intimate lives of "single again" older people, as there is a paucity of data on late life romantic relationships of men and women following widowhood or divorce.

As we age we typically feel that we are the same person with the same desires and failings. We fall in love, experience the joy of acceptance and the pain of rejection, treasure our fantasies and fond memories. This idea was famously expressed by J. B. Priestley when asked about his feelings on his eightieth birthday:

> ...it was as though walking down Shaftesbury Avenue as a fairly young man, I was suddenly kidnapped, rushed into a theatre and made up to don the grey hair, the wrinkles and other attributes of age, then wheeled on-stage. ... Behind the appearance of

age I am the same person, with the same thoughts, as when I was younger. (Quoted in Fennell et al., 1988: 15)

Yet the reality of how people feel in themselves is not reflected and supported by cultural norms. Elderly people are commonly supposed to be different from the rest of the population, sexually less eligible and probably also sexless beings. For instance, in a recent authoritative sex survey in the UK (the NATSAL 2000 survey, Johnson et al., 2001), no one above the age of forty-four was included in the sample, presumably because they were supposed not to have sex, or their sexual behavior was of less interest, less valid, than that of younger adults.

The first ever nationwide random sample survey of the sexual behavior of an adult population was conducted in Sweden in 1967 (Zetterberg, 2002). Although his was in many ways an exemplary study, Zetterberg was not alone among sex researchers in taking age sixty as the higher age cut-off for his sample. He noted however that his sixty-year-olds were sexually active and that "it is clear that one must go higher up the age groups to fix the point at which sexual activity stops" (2002: 145). Like subsequent authors Zetterberg found that the most important determinant of sexual activity is not age, but having access to a regular partner. It is here, of course, that later life may take its toll, through the break-up and dissolution of relationships or the illness of a partner. As Zetterberg commented, "progressively more people lose their lifelong partner; one becomes a widow or a widower and then allows sexual activity to cease" (ibid).

In a more recent survey in Sweden, more than thirty years later, partially replicating Zetterberg's work (Lewin et al., 2000), the sample boundaries were extended to age seventy-four and the authors comment that "it is hardly possible to determine" this hypothetical "point at which sexual activity stops." For those aged over seventy at the time of this recent survey, more than half had had sexual intercourse during the previous year (Lewin et al., 2000: 62). In all acts of heterosexual intercourse in the whole Swedish population taken together, the average age of the man was six years older than that of the woman. Given the attrition of males in the older age ranges, if this continues to be a powerful norm – that the man should be older than the woman – there could clearly be social-structural difficulties for women who had lost partners, if they wanted to continue heterosexual activity. In contemporary culture, however, there is scant support for the idea that older people should or should want to be sexually active in later life.

Perhaps what we are observing here is the phenomenon known as "cultural lag," where cultural ideas have not caught up with real changes in social behavior. Lewin et al. noted that elderly Swedes were as likely to enjoy penetrative vaginal sex as their younger counterparts. Any diminution of sexual activity, if it occurred, took place at least ten years later than in the earlier 1967 Swedish survey.

It is impossible to isolate people's ideas and behavior in the area of love, intimacy and sex from the wider cultural heritage, wherever in the world we grow up and live. In Europe and America the inherited sex-negativity of Christianity and the power of romantic love ideology have combined to leave deep cultural stains. They make us comfortable to think of heterosexual sex in relation to stable pair-bonded relationships between adults of child-rearing age, particularly those who are in love, or professed themselves in love near the start of their relationship.

If culture delimits what relationships are permissible and when, biological or physiological ageing clearly also has some impact (but only some) on the way people think and behave. For instance, the urgency of desire may diminish somewhat, rather than desire itself. With age, also, more people suffer age-related illnesses such as diabetes, stroke, dementia or the effects of long-term alcohol damage, which in turn impact upon sexual function. We are accustomed to think there are gender-related differences in sexuality (crudely put as men being always keen on sex and women never having been as interested and happier to give it up). Older people might reflect these norms more strongly than younger people, having grown to maturity at a time when social attitudes to sexuality were "restrictive" (following Zetterberg) rather than "permissive." The very oldest women in the population are those most likely to have had only one lifetime sexual partner and to have been "initiated" into sexual activity by their husbands. They are least likely to have either active or passive experience of a wide range of sexual acts and to be most restrictive in their outlook on sexual matters. Sex researchers in Europe have noted large changes in recent years in young women's sexual behavior, leading to a growing "convergence" on many indicators among young adults of both genders (Hubert et al., 1998; Kontula and Haavio-Mannila, 1995; Lewin et al., 2000; Wellings et al., 1994). Today's young women, in later life, will have very different sexual histories from their grandmothers and perhaps a correspondingly different outlook.

More recently, sex researchers have begun to comment on the positive and life-enhancing aspects of sexuality (Fennell, 2002; Kontula and Haavio-Mannila, 1995; Lewin et al., 2000). Zetterberg writes of sex as "an under-exploited reservoir of joy" in the human population (2002: 29, 86). Having an intimate, confiding relationship (often, but not exclusively, with a lover) is an acknowledged antidote to depression (Brown and Harris, 1978) and medical research has begun to acknowledge the positive, life-extending benefits of hugging, touching, skin-caressing, and even orgasm (e.g. Smith et al., 1997).

For social and cultural reasons, these forms of physical expression are generally only permitted in "approved" relationships between appropriate partners. Approved sexual partners should be similar to one another in age: if there is an age difference, the male should be the older of the two. Relationships should be long-term and involve sexual exclusiveness. Infidelity and relationship breakdown nonetheless occur and many people lose a partner after the age of fifty through death, women (statistically) far more so than men. Quite short-term, perhaps serial, relationships appear to be becoming the norm in younger sections of the population. How do people behave in later life with regard to relationship breakdown and partner change? Widows and widowers in former times (particularly men who lost their wives in childbirth, or when children were young) have always had a propensity to remarry and there have always been strong economic reasons for people to share households and pool expenses. How do older people today think and behave in relation to partner change today? This is part of the new social territory that this volume seeks to map.

Most of the chapters in this volume arise from an invited symposium on "Repartnering After Late Life Widowhood: The Gendered Perspective" at the 17th Congress of the International Association of Gerontology (IAG) held in Vancouver, Canada in 2001. However, although the principal focus is on widowhood and new relationships, for the publication we have widened the remit to include that burgeoning population, in the Western world particularly, of older divorced men and women. The object of the symposium was to bring together a wide range of distinguished international academics interested in a hitherto neglected research area, that of new partnership formation in later life. Choices and constraints which influence decisions about new romantic relationships after divorce or the loss of a spouse are explored and how these might intersect with age, gender and culture. It could be argued that researchers in northern Europe, particularly Scandinavia and the Netherlands currently dominate this field, hence their high visibility in this svolume. Nevertheless, chapters from Asia, North America, and the United Kingdom serve to offer cross-cultural perspectives.

This is new territory and territory also which is changing, as our authors note. Studies are typically small-scale and of limited generalisability. Comparisons, for instance, of widowed Chinese, Malays, and Indians in Singapore with whites in "permissive" societies such as Sweden, Holland, and the UK—as contrasted again with a morally conservative area such as New Brunswick in Canada—show considerable cultural variability in what is regarded as appropriate behavior. There is also acknowledgement that norms are changing, in some parts of the world faster than others. Successive cohorts of elderly people are likely to show more extensive changes in a few years' time than others, in part because of their different cultural histories, their experience, for instance, of the perceived sexual revolution of the "permissive Sixties" and of secularisation, where these occurred.

In thinking about people "repartnering" (or not) in later life, we must also acknowledge the impact of their former relationships. The loss of a long-term, perhaps life-long, partner has a major impact and the relationship might be viewed as irreplaceable. The loss of a partner through death may have been preceded by a period of long-term caring in which sexual activity has diminished through illness and also altered one's perspective on what such relationships may entail. Perhaps as many as a quarter of relationships are experienced as abusive, unhappy or sexually unfulfilling, which might temper anyone's enthusiasm for a repeat. A first consideration, therefore, in repartnering is likely to be the nature and quality of a previous relationship. If very good, and of high emotional intensity, a previous partner might be regarded as irreplaceable. If poor, it might condition the individual against seeking a repeat and reduce the expectation of being able to fare better. Alternatively, if the dissolution of marriage was the result of divorce (where it can be assumed there had been high levels of conflict and/or unhappiness for at least one of the partners), the individual may consider that he or she might have "better luck next time."

Another consideration, is the quality of life currently experienced by the widowed person. Carr and Utz in chapter 2 reveal that although widowed mothers receive more instrumental support from adult children than do men, they tend to maintain their role as the family's emotional and expressive caretaker. In terms of loving, and being loved, this exchange may be sufficient to fulfil a widow's emotional needs. Carr and Utz report that a man, on the other hand, is not only likely to have become more emotionally bonded to his wife in later life as a result of the post-retirement diminishing circle of friends, but that his adult children are less likely to assist him in household tasks. This apparently greater emotional and instrumental need for companionship may influence a man's decision to seek another partner.

The environing cultural and social background will also influence whether or not individuals even think of repartnering, let alone do anything about it. As Mehta shows for Singapore (chapter 8), older people in Asia are not supposed to have biological (sexual) needs after their procreative period is behind them, the very idea is culturally taboo. Cultural considerations, ideas about relationships, are reinforced by social sanctions including the threat of ridicule or ostracism. Other relatives, particularly adult children, may be hostile to the surviving parent "replacing" the deceased one.

Various of our authors consider "push and pull" factors, or the pros and cons of relationships, whether new or old. Loneliness and isolation may be an obvious stimulus to escape from a given situation; someone to have and to hold may be a "pull." As Parkes (1972) noted in his classic study of bereavement, widowed people feel more vulnerable and *are* more vulnerable: there is strength in numbers, and in recent years the appropriate number to form a relationship has been two. Stevens (chapter 3) very helpfully lists some of the positive attractions of a domestic relationship, including the anxiety-reducing ability to bounce ideas off a partner.

In our relativistic age, however, nothing can be regarded as an unmixed blessing. Relationships have costs as well as benefits and various authors elaborate what some of these may be. Women, in particular, may not want to perpetuate the "unequal division of household labor" which they may have experienced in a previous marriage, as Ghazanfareeon Karlsson and Borell point out (chapter 1). If women think only in terms of an older male partner, they may themselves display ageing stereotypes and not fancy an "old man."

Older women, more commonly than older men, may regard sex as the "price" of a relationship, one which they no longer wish to pay.

For men, it may be thought, the equation might be different – a new woman might offer the advantages (to them) of an unequal division of domestic labor and the prospect of someone to care for them when (as statistically they must expect) their health fails. For men, sex might be a bonus rather than a cost. Moore and Stratton (chapter 7) look at the "current woman" in older widowers' lives. They note that these relationships involve social activity, friendship and filial-type companionship, as well as romantic liaisons, with or without sexual intimacy. They note that older men who desire a new intimate relationship tend to seek and enter a new partnership within months of the death of their spouse.

Suppose someone in later life does wish to launch him or herself back into the relationship market – a cost in itself, if there has been a long period of unfamiliarity with the process, a lack of practice and of exposure to competition – eligibility and social structural factors come into play, as Davidson shows (chapter 4). Propinquity and similarity-with-difference are important factors in the formation of relationships. Many writers have concluded that women would be at an increasing structural disadvantage in later life in mate-competition given the dwindling number of unattached males, particular if women assume that partners will be five to six years older than themselves.

Davidson's model shows how access to health, wealth and social networks impact on the likelihood of new partnership formation in later life. In men, says Davidson, wealth may offset other disadvantages (particularly poor health), but this is not true in women, where good health is a greater resource for selection into a new partnership. It is well documented that we are living longer, and are generally in better health than previous generations, until the last year or so before death (Fries, 1980). There is a correlation between health and wealth in men: the wealthier the man, the healthier he tends to be and the longer he tends to live (Courtney, 2000). Women, by contrast, although on average living longer than men, are more likely to suffer from longstanding limiting illness such as arthritis or diabetes. Since good health is one determinant of the degree of sexual activity (Deck et al., 2002), it could be argued that older men are more likely to seek an intimate relationship after the dissolution of their previous partnership.

But it would be a mistake to overstate gender stereotypes. Living together with anyone requires delicate adjustments and accommodations of all sorts for both sexes. The pain and difficulty of this, what we might think of as the labor of love, can be more than some men will contemplate. Where wealth assets are unequal, both men and women may be wary of possible "gold-digging" in a potential partner. As van den Hoonaard points out (chapter 6), norms regarding interactions between men and women are ambiguous, and both widows and widowers at times need to find creative new ways to interact safely with the opposite sex in order to avoid misunderstandings both about their interest in remarriage or their desire or lack of desire to engage in intimate activity.

Suppose a pair get together, what then? In the Western world, most older people live in one-generation households and after the death of a spouse, live alone in the marital home. The authors from Europe report that older divorced and widowed persons are increasingly opting for flexible partner bonds such as unmarried cohabitation and Living Apart Together (LAT) relationships—where partners do not actually live together—rather than remarriage. Ghazanfareeon Karlsson and Borell (chapter 1) describe LAT relationships as a comparatively new phenomenon within the older population. The trend is confirmed by Stevens (chapter 3) and by de Jong Gierveld (chapter 5) who examine the motivations and pathways for choice of domicile in a new relationship. They conclude that the arrangement can offer "the best of both worlds": intimacy with autonomy, companionship with independence.

Independence is not an issue within the cultural climate described by Mehta (chapter 8). In Singapore, as in many parts of Asia and in the Asian diaspora, it is more common to assimilate a widowed person into an extended family household. Mehta found that a large majority of the older widowed people had negative perceptions of remarriage. But even within the Singaporean community, there were ethnic differences. In the Malay culture, remarriage was more acceptable: among the Chinese and Indians remarriage still carried a stigma.

In conclusion, as our authors reveal, gender, culture, family expectations, social mores and importantly, self-agency, contribute to choices and constraints in establishing a new partnership whether not at all, non co-residential or living together. What is revealed from this set of chapters, is a complex picture of relationship and friendship matrices which transcend the simple dichotomy of whether an older person wishes or otherwise to establish another relationship after the loss of a partner.

References

Brown, G.W., and Harris, T. (1978). *Social origins of depression: A study of psychiatric disorders in women.* London: Tavistock.

Courtney, W. H. (2000). Constructions of masculinity and their influence on men's well-being: A theory of gender and health. *Social Science and Medicine* 50, 1385-1401.

Deck, R., Kohlmann, T., and Jordan, M. (2002). Health-related quality of life in old age: Preliminary report on the male perspective. *The Aging Male* 5(2), 87-97.

Fennell, G., Phillipson, C., and Evers, H. (1st pub 1988). *The sociology of old age.* Milton Keynes: Open University Press.

Fennell, G. (2002). A landmark in the history of sex research: Introduction to translation of Hans L. Zetterberg, *Sexual Life in Sweden.* New Brunswick, NJ: Transaction Publishers.

Fries J. (1980). Aging, natural death and the compression of morbidity. *New England Journal of Medicine* 303(3), 130-135

Hubert M., Bajor, N., and Sandfort, T. (Eds.). (1998). *Sexual behaviour and HIV/AIDS in Europe.* London: UCL.

Johnson, A.M., Mercer, C.H., Erens, B., Copas, A.J., McManus, S., Wellings, K., Fenton, K.A., Korovessis, C., Macdowall, W., Nanchahal, K., Purdon, S., and Field, J. (2001). Sexual behavior in Britain: Partnerships, practices, and HIV risk behaviors. *The Lancet* 358 (9296) 1835-42.

Kontula, O., and Haavio-Mannila, E. (1995). *Sexual pleasures: Enhancement of sex life in Finland 1971-1992.* Aldershot: Dartmouth.

Lewin, B. (Ed.) (2000). *Sex in Sweden: On the Swedish sexual life 1996*, Stockholm: National Institute of Public Health.

Parkes, C.M. (1972). *Bereavement, Studies of grief in adult life.* London: Tavistock.

Smith, G.D., Frankel, S., and Yarnell, J. (1997). Sex and death, are they related? Findings from the Caerphilly cohort study. *British Medical Journal* 315, 1641-1644.

Wellings, K., Field, J., Johnson, A., and Wadsworth, J. (1994). *Sexual behaviour in Britain: The national survey of sexual attitudes and lifestyles.* Harmondsworth: Penguin.

Zetterberg, H.L. (2002). *Sexual life in Sweden.* Translated with a new Introduction by Graham Fennell. (1st published (1969) as *Om Sexuallivet i Sverige*). New Brunswick, NJ: Transaction Publishers.

1

Intimacy and Autonomy, Gender and Ageing: Living Apart Together

Sofie Ghazanfareeon Karlsson and Klas Borell

Contemporary family life and intimate relationships are characterized by a new and increasing heterogeneity. In the growing body of research on this differentiation of family patterns and practices, the role of older people has largely been ignored. Studies of the family life of older people often deal with the adjustments that take place between couples when their children have left home or with the attempts of widows and widowers to come to terms with a life without their lifelong partners (for research reviews, see Allen et al., 2000; Borell, 2001; Brubaker, 1990; Goldscheider, 1990). When, on rare occasions, the important changes that have occurred in family life and intimate relationships are recognized, they usually deal with the indirect effect these may have on older people, such as the consequences of their children's divorces for their roles as grandparents (see, for example, Cherlin and Furstenberg, 1986). For each new cohort of the ageing population this omission becomes less defensible: to an increasing extent the "young old" (sixty-five to seventy-four years of age) in particular are prime movers in the process of the differentiation of family forms and practices.

This is especially evident in Sweden, one of the countries where the differentiation of family forms has progressed farthest. The change in the proportion of divorcees to widows and widowers in the age group sixty-five to sixty-nine, that is, the youngest of the "young old," illustrates this. While the improved health of this age group has meant that the number of widows and widowers has decreased by almost half in the period 1968 to 2000, the number of divorcees has more than quadrupled in the same time. Since 1997 it has become more usual in the age group sixty-five to sixty-nine to be a divorcee than to be a widow or widower (Swedish Central Bureau of Statistics, 1968–2000, authors' analysis). Another manifestation of the change in intimate relationships and family forms amongst older people is the increasing number who cohabit without getting married. Between the census years 1975 and 1990 (the latest census year in Sweden), the percentage of cohabitants in the oldest registered group (sixty to sixty-four years of age) doubled in relation to the total number of cohabitants, from 2.8 percent to 5.9 percent (Swedish Central Bureau of Statistics, 1992a).

One of the least researched contributions of older people to the restructuring of contemporary Swedish intimate relationships and family life is the establishment of lasting intimate relationships which do not include a mutual home, that is, an alternative to different forms of cohabitation, which is sometimes referred to as Living Apart Together (henceforth "LAT relationships").

Beyond the Boundaries of a Single Household

A house or an apartment, be it rented or owned, is often assumed to constitute the setting in which intimate family relations take place. But a common feature of several of the emerging patterns of family and intimate relationships, is that they—in different ways and to different degrees—challenge the link between a single household and family life that is often taken for granted. In commuter marriages, usually a temporary arrangement where career development is identified as the primary motive, partners work in different locations during the week and share a residence only on weekends (Winfield, 1985). Gay and lesbian families do not share a particular family form, but members of these *families of choice* often belong to two or more households (Weston, 1991). Networks of support and exchange between divorced men and women can also be included in these spatially flexible family constellations. Some authors speak about recombinant or binuclear families, where the children regularly move between the households of their divorced parents and maintain a double membership of two households (Ahron and Rodgers, 1987; Cherlin, 1999; Maccoby and Mnookin, 1992).

LAT relationships are probably the least studied of these new intimate multi-household constellations, and the LAT relationships of older people have hardly been studied at all (but see Borell, 2001; Borell and Ghazanfareeon Karlsson, 2000). However, it is clear that LAT relationships constitute an increasingly popular alternative to cohabitation (with or without marriage) in Sweden. Approximately 4 percent of all the adults in Sweden live in LAT relationships and even given the uncertain nature of the data, the proportion appears to be highest among the "young old" (Levin and Trost, 2001). The aim of this study is to examine LAT relationships between older couples and the motives that might lie behind their choice to live in multi-household relationships.

The Ontological Status of LAT Relationships

Even though it has recently increased to some degree, remarriage is unusual between older couples in most countries in the Western world (Burch, 1990; Steitz and Welker, 1991). The difficulties involved in finding a new partner are only part of the explanation. Previous research has shown that older women are doubtful about marriage, not only because they run the risk of becoming "locked into" a traditional marriage role, but also, and more specifically, because they do not want to run the risk of eventually becoming a "nurse" to an often older man (Lopata, 1996). This does not necessarily mean that they are therefore uninterested in intimate relationships. Even though the empirical data are limited at present, a number of studies indicate that there is a growing trend amongst older single people towards finding new forms of pair bonding that allow for long-term intimacy without necessarily involving marriage or cohabitation (Bulcroft and Bulcroft, 1991; Bulcroft and O'Connor, 1986; Talbott, 1998; Wilson, 1995). Even though this trend can be identified in several countries in the Western world, there are nevertheless cultural differences that should be noted.

One notable feature of American studies of intimate relationships amongst older people is the absence of an established terminology to describe long-term relationships that do not involve cohabitation. When interviewees refer to intimate relationships of this kind they often borrow terms that relate to youth culture, which they then have to qualify or delimit. For instance, they use expressions such as "going steady" or "dating" as approximations, since no more suitable terms exist (e.g., Bulcroft and O'Connor, 1986). In Sweden, on the other hand, a term for long-term relations between two adults who are not cohabitants has existed for the last twenty years, namely *särbo* (where *sär* stands for "apart" and *bo* for "to live"). This linguistic differentiation is probably of far greater significance than is at first apparent. The acceptance of the concept *särbo* gives an ontological status to a type of relationship that involves separate domiciles, but which is not a transitional form leading to cohabitation, within or outside wedlock. By naming the concept, and thereby at least roughly defining it in relation to other family forms or intimate relationships, this type of relationship becomes a distinct alternative about which people can consciously form an opinion or make a choice (Borell, 2001).

Nevertheless, it is naturally important to stress that LAT relationships in Sweden are not institutionalized to the same degree as marriage (or, for that matter, unmarried cohabitation). While married life tends to follow certain articulated and generally accepted patterns, partners in LAT relationships have few conventions or established patterns of relating to one another on which to fall back. They have to construct their own set of rules and roles, without the help of more specific cultural patterns that apply to this type of relationship. This first study of LAT relationships amongst older people aims to focus on these rules and roles, that is, to examine how older LAT partners organize their lives together, and how they define the commitment they have to one another. Furthermore, it aims to examine the motives behind their choice of this particular form of relationship.

Method

Individuals who form LAT relationships are not registered in any official statistics. They are part of a "hidden population," the exact size and boundaries of which are unknown. It was therefore impossible to make a statistically representative sample of older couples living in LAT relationships. In view of this we have chosen to obtain a sample through advertising. Naturally, one of the disadvantages of this approach is that the researcher lacks control over who responds in terms of how representative they are. In order to compensate for this problem as much as possible we have chosen to place the advertisements in local newspapers, which are read in Sweden by a large proportion of the ageing population (Hadenius and Weibull, 2000). In total, nine advertisements were placed in the local newspapers of three different regions, which together represent both rural and urban areas (for a methodological discussion on sampling of hidden populations, see Lee, 1993).

The advertisement, which was identical in all the different papers, sought individuals and couples of sixty years of age and over, to take part in a study of LAT relationships (*särboende*) amongst older people. As a result of this advertising 116 individuals took part in the survey, including eighteen couples. All of the respondents had heterosexual LAT relationships. There was a considerable range of ages in the sample—from sixty to ninety years of age—but the majority (52 percent) fell into the group of the young old, while the median age in the whole group was seventy. The vast majority were retired, but about 10 percent were still working. Slightly more women than men were interviewed, the sample containing 57 percent women and 43 percent men. Almost half of the respondents were divorced and approximately 40 percent were widows or widowers. The vast majority of the respondents had children of their own (91 percent) and grandchildren (85 percent). Over 50 percent of the participants lived in medium-sized towns, but about 20 percent lived in rural and 20 percent in metropolitan areas.

The sample is not representative of the older population at large in two important respects. First, the sample has a considerably higher level of education. If we limit ourselves to a comparison between the age group sixty-five to seventy-four in our sample with data about the same age group taken from the entire population, the percentage with a low education (without senior high school or higher qualifications) is much greater in the general public (76 percent compared with 44 percent) and the percentage with higher education (at college or university level) is more than three times greater in our sample (49 percent compared with 15 percent in the general public) (Swedish Central Bureau of Statistics, 2000b). Second, the sample is characterized by relatively better health. Over 80 percent of the respondents between sixty-five and seventy-four years of age in the sample claim that their health is good to very good, while representative data from an equivalent group of the general public shows that only 65 percent of them claim this (Swedish Central Bureau of Statistics, 2000c). Differences of this sort must of course be treated with caution and must be seen in the light of the method of sampling that has been employed. It is probable that healthy, active, and well-educated older individuals are more likely to respond to an advertisement asking for participation in a survey than other older people. However, the extent of the differentiation, as well as the fact that the advertising was done in a way that should have reduced social bias, indicate that there really is a difference between the groups, that is, those that choose to live in LAT relationships are those who are healthier and have a higher level of education.

In the following discussion, data from this survey are presented together with qualitative data from a previous pilot study which involved in-depth face-to-face interviews with fourteen men and women. These interviews were usually carried out in the respondents' homes and took, on average, seventy minutes to complete. Pseudonyms are used for individuals throughout the paper.

Living Apart Together in Old Age

LAT relationships among senior citizens are in certain respects not a uniform experience. The partners may live on the same block or far apart; the distance between the domiciles of the partners in the survey sample varies from virtually nil (the couple live in the same apartment block) to 450 kilometers (with a median distance of 6 kilometers). The partners in all the relationships studied keep in touch with each other by telephone on a more or less daily basis, but the time actually spent together varies; 36 percent meet almost every day, 51 percent a couple of times a week, and 12 percent twice a month or even more seldom. All the respondents see their relationship as long-term relationships, but the length of time they say they have been LAT partners varies widely, from twenty-eight years to one year (with a median length of six years). In spite of this variation relatively clear patterns emerge, both regarding the motives for living in LAT relationships and in the rules and roles that have been adopted by the partners.

Autonomy

Many older couples are obliged to live apart against their will, because of changes brought about by illness: one spouse may be institutionalized while the other still lives in the community (Kaplan, 2001). In contrast to these involuntarily separated couples, LAT partners choose of their own free will to live in separate households, that is, to "live apart together." However, it would be mistaken to assume that this is a result of LAT relationships being less focused on intimacy or less emotionally close than other relationships between men and women. Both our survey data and our in-depth interviews indicate that LAT partners see their relationships as deeply intimate in the broadest sense of the word, that is, they represent mutual trust, understanding, and the sharing of confidences. A seventy-five-year-old woman, Carin, explains that when she became older she felt a strong need for a close relationship

> that can provide intimacy. I think that we need one another now when we are old ... My partner is my support and I think he feels the same way ... If, for example, I feel sick sometimes, I can call him and tell him about it. It is so good to have someone who will listen to me at times like that.

A sixty-seven-year-old woman, Sally, gives a similar picture of the situation:

> My partner ... is fantastic at backing me up! He listens to me when I read poetry and when I sing in the choir.... He cares about me, quite simply, in a wonderful way. When I was taken ill one evening a couple of years ago I called him up and he came over and stayed with me overnight. My children live so far away, so it is my partner I turn to if I have any problems. It was the same when he was taken ill. It was me he turned to, first of all.

Faithfulness is also a central part of these relationships. One man, Eric, says that he often goes out dancing and there he meets other women:

> Some of the women show a certain interest in me, but no, I never let it go beyond that point. My partner and I meet every day, so it would be disastrous for both of us. Moreover, she has warned me: if I go out with anyone else, that will be it!

What is it that motivates these older couples to choose to live in a multi-household relationship rather than as married or unmarried cohabitants?

The results of the survey do not give a unified picture of these motives. Instead a pattern appears that indicates a considerable difference between the answers of men and women. In general one can say that the women tend to give more unambiguous and unanimous answers about their motives for choosing this particular kind of relationship. This pattern alone gives an important clue to understanding the situation: it suggests that it is the women rather than the men that are the driving force behind the choice to live as LAT partners.

Men, like the women, repudiate the suggestion that their choice of a LAT relationship is motivated by financial considerations or is based on unhappy experiences from earlier relationships. On the other hand, significantly more women than men mention the difficulty involved in adapting to a new partner's habits or ways and the practical difficulties of living together (for example, that one of the partners is a heavy smoker while the other is allergic to smoke; or that neither of them wants to sell their home). But the gender disparity is above all evident regarding two further motives, namely the importance of having a home of one's own and secondly the importance of being freed from duties that would arise if one was married (see table 1.1). These two latter motives revolve largely around *autonomy*.

The autonomy theme is even more apparent in the face-to-face interviews we conducted. In these interviews, women emphasize the fact that LAT relationships mean that they can combine intimacy with what they repeatedly refer to as their strong desire to "be by themselves" or "live their own lives." Retaining a home of their own is an essential factor. It is a place in which personal control is ensured and optimized; a boundary-making resource which these women draw on to balance their need for privacy and time alone with their need for intimacy and closeness.

Table 1.1

Men and Women's Motives for Choosing a LAT-Relationship				
Items	N (m:f)	Median (m:f)	Mean rank (m:f)	P
Importance of having a home of one's own	(50 : 63)	(7 : 10)	(46.95 : 64.98)	.003
Importance of economic factors	(50 : 64)	(0 : 0)	(53.26 : 60.81)	n.s
Importance of negative experience from earlier relationships	(50 : 63)	(0 : 1)	(53.25 : 59.98)	n.s
Importance of being freed from duties that would arise if one was married	(49 : 63)	(4 : 8)	(47.24 : 63.70)	.007
Importance of being accessible to children and grandchildren	(48 : 60)	(1.5 : 5)	(48.94 : 58.95)	n.s
Importance of own habits	(50 : 64)	(5 : 5)	(53.08 : 60.95)	n.s
Importance of practical reasons concerning living arrangements	(50 : 64)	(7 : 8.5)	(50.72 : 62.80)	.048
Importance of the habits of partner	(50 : 64)	(2.5 : 5)	(49.65 : 63.63)	.023

Each item is scaled from 0 (no importance) to 10 (great importance). The Mann-Whitney U-test is used to test the null hypothesis that the mean rank of men and women is identical.

Patricia, sixty-two, says:

> Having a home of my own lets me feel I am deciding for myself and that I don't have to consider other people. It wouldn't work if we lived together. Then I couldn't say: "It's time for you to go."

Throughout the interviews, women describe their own home and their self-imposed single status as a privilege, and marriage or other forms of cohabitation as a loss of this privilege. Anne, seventy, thinks that it

> feels good to be able to take it easy a few days a week and to be yourself after having been married for so long and having been responsible for the home. Then, somehow, you were tied and couldn't do as you wanted.

Glory, seventy-five, although she meets her partner almost daily, says that she

> needs to be alone, at least during the morning. Then I do the washing or baking. These things are more easily done when I am alone. I take it easy. I can organize the morning as I wish: that's what's so wonderful.

Helen, sixty-six, states that her friends sometimes try to encourage her to move in with her partner for financial reasons, but she says

> I would rather be less well off and live alone. Then I can get up when I want and eat when I want. I explain this to my friends and after listening to me for a while they say, "How wise of you, I would also like to live like that."

Household Labor and Collective Resources

The women involved in the LAT relationships that we have studied value their own home as a means of protection against the gendered duties implicit in a marriage. Having a home of one's own acts as a demarcation for the distribution of domestic labor. "*His home is his, and my home is mine,*" says one of the women interviewed. This does not mean that the LAT relationships entered into by older people in all respects nullify a traditional division of labor. Certainly relationships exist in which partners visit each other's homes in turn and, to give just one example, take turns preparing meals. However, as our survey data show, it is more common that the couple meet in the woman's house and that she also prepares the meals on these occasions: 18 percent of the participants say that they generally meet in the man's home, 35 percent that they alternate between each other's homes, and 45 percent that they most often meet in the woman's home (which is also where they usually spend the night together). It is also usual that the woman cooks the meals they eat together, even when they take turns to meeting in each other's homes or meet in the man's home, and that the man often repairs things in the woman's home.

Despite the existence of this traditional division of household labor, LAT relationships provide a vital boundary-setting resource for women. The face-to-face interview with Patricia illustrates this. She describes how she usually prepares the food when she meets her partner, but emphasizes that this does not mean that she is prepared to take on responsibility for her partner's home:

> We each do our own cleaning in our own homes. I can moan at him a little and say that he should clean the windows or do other things, but I would never do them for him.

A consequence of having separate households is that the couples also have separate finances. A married couple who live together usually have a joint private economy and over the years acquire a number of shared resources (house, car, holiday home, etc.). The LAT partners we studied all have their own private household economies and very few have many joint resources. Usually they divide current expenses (often for the meals they eat together) between them (77 percent), although in some cases the men pay for the ingredients, perhaps as a way of "compensating" for the woman's work in preparing the meal. Most participants (79 percent) have no joint savings of any kind. Those who do save together with their LAT partner are all saving towards some specific goal, such as a planned holiday together. There are also very few that say that they have shared possessions: over 85 percent of the respondents say that they do not have any shared possessions at all. In the cases where a couple does have joint ownership it is never of expensive items, such as cars. A typical example is that one of the LAT partners owns a holiday home where the couple spends time together, but they might own things such as the household utensils there jointly.

An interesting, and counterintuitive finding, is that joint ownership and saving does not appear to increase in relation to the duration of the relationship. Relationships that have stretched over a period of eight years or more do not seem to be characterized by a greater degree of joint ownership than relationships of less than eight years (and the shorter relationships actually report a significantly *higher* degree of joint saving than the longer ones). These results indicate that LAT relationships do not tend to lead to an increasing amount of common commitments or, expressed in another way, become more "marriage-like."

Future Care

The new LAT relationships between older people do not lack mutual commitments, but these commitments would seem to deal mostly with the giving and receiving of emotional support. However, we ought to bear in mind that the majority of the people we have interviewed are not just "young-old" but are also in relatively good health. An interesting question is therefore the issue of the way in which LAT partners see how the commitment between them will develop when one of them becomes seriously ill.

The participants in the survey were asked to envisage a future scenario where their partner becomes seriously ill and try to describe how they would handle this situation. The answers to this question show that only a few would refuse to take care of their partner in any way, and practically nobody would end the relationship because of their partner's ill health. Most of them, however, envisage taking on a more or less limited degree of care for their partner. They can consider caring for an ill partner a few days a week or a few hours a day, but not full-time.

It is important to emphasize that this result should not be interpreted entirely on the basis of the form of intimate relationship that the individual has chosen. It is also influenced by the fact that Sweden, with its welfare system, still offers its citizens high-quality public care and service in their old age. In spite of the cutbacks that have taken place within the old age care sector during the 1990s people in Sweden still have high expectations of good care in their old age (Blomberg et al., 2000; Swedish National Board of Health and Welfare, 2000).

Nevertheless, there are important differences between the views of women and men (see table 1.2). Significantly more men than women are prepared to take care of their partner for a few hours every day, and significantly more men than women can even think of taking care of their partners full-time if necessary.

There are various ways in which the difference between the attitude of men and women to taking care of their partners in the future can be interpreted. However, an obvious starting point would seem to be the systematic gender differences that exist in the care of the

Table 1.2

Men and Women's Attitudes to Future Care of LAT Partner

Items	N (m:f)	Median (m:f)	Mean rank (m:f)	P
Would consider taking care of partner for some months if he/she were seriously ill	(49: 65)	(8.4: 7.7)	(60.67: 55.11)	n.s
Would consider taking care of partner any length of time	(49: 64)	(6.6: 4.8)	(65.41: 50.56)	.016
Would not consider taking care of partner if he/she were seriously ill	(47: 65)	(1.9: 2.6)	(53.37: 58.76)	n.s
Would end the relationship if partner became seriously ill	(49: 65)	(0.8: 1.3)	(56.48: 58.27)	n.s
Would consider taking care of partner a few days a week	(49: 64)	(6.9: 5.9)	(63.21: 52.24)	n.s
Would consider taking care of partner a few hours a day	(48: 64)	(6.9: 5.5)	(63.57: 51.20)	.039
Would consider taking care of partner 24 hours a day	(48: 65)	(3.7: 2.6)	(61.18: 53.92)	n.s
Would move to live with partner if he/she became seriously ill	(49: 65)	(4.6 : 3.1)	(64.06: 52.55)	n.s

Each item is scaled from 0 (completely disagree) to 10 (completely agree). The Mann-Whitney U-test is used to test the null hypothesis that the mean rank of men and women is identical.

older people. In Sweden, as in most countries, the old age care is, to a disproportionate degree, the province of women, especially wives, and, historically, women's unpaid and often inconspicuous care for husbands has been taken for granted as part of the marriage contract. The women who choose to form a LAT relationship no doubt see the risk of becoming imprisoned in a traditional marital role (and ultimately of taking on new caring commitments in their old age) as a major issue—and have therefore chosen a form of intimate relationship that does not involve either marriage or unmarried cohabitation. Thus, although both men and women in the study were asked to say to what degree they would hypothetically be prepared to care for their partner, it was the women much more than the men who had seriously considered this aspect of the relationship, as it relates to an issue of which they are fully aware, and which had undoubtedly been a major factor in their decision to "live apart together."

The restructuring of old age care that has taken place in Sweden in the past decade can throw some further light on the differences between the attitude of men and women to care of their partner in the future. The number of senior citizens having access to social services has decreased as the most needy in the ageing population have been prioritized and in certain municipalities it has become increasingly difficult for older couples living under the same roof to get assistance (Swedish National Board of Health and Welfare, 2000). *"I'll do everything I can to help and support my partner when he becomes ill and really old,"* says Ruth. But at the same time she adds that so long as she appears to have her *"feet under the table, then the welfare services won't do their bit."* In other words Ruth, like many of the women interviewed, sees a home of her own as a protection against potential demands made by the society that she, as a partner, should provide the care and attention that would otherwise be the responsibility of the local authority's welfare service.

Discussion and Conclusions

LAT relationships, that is, lasting intimate relationships which do not include a mutual household, are no doubt among the least researched of the new forms of family and intimate relationships that have emerged over the past decades. Moreover, the LAT relationships of older people have hardly been studied at all. In order to understand what makes LAT relationships of older people distinctive, a comparison can be made between them and marriage, which is still the most highly institutionalized form of heterosexual partnership.

Although they have differing theoretical approaches and conceptual perspectives, Becker (1960, 1981), Johnson (1991), and Johnson and Caughlin (1999) have all noted the complex nature of the commitments that married couples have towards one another. Marriage today is often based upon romantic love and attraction and also tends to include a sense of moral obligation to one another. But the bond between spouses also includes ties that can be described as structural commitments, that is, ties that imply that a relationship has to continue because of joint investments that have been made. These structural ties—that can keep a marriage together, even when the relationship has lost its mutual emotional and moral bonds—are multiple. Over the years a couple acquire a number of jointly owned resources (of which their shared home is usually the most expensive investment). If they have children together, they are bound together through this common relationship to a third party. Marriages with children also usually develop over time a considerable and often increasingly specialized division of labor, which also increases the couple's mutual interdependence. Moreover, through marriage the couple become interwoven with each other's networks of kin and friends, which also leads to long-term and complex loyalties and commitments. Furthermore, although contemporary family life is characterized by increasing differentiation, the still strong institutional and cultural sanctioning of marriage constitutes yet another element of the structural bonds. Marriage is a legally sanctioned form of cohabitation and it is also a type of relationship for which there is a clearly defined cultural praxis.

Marriage can of course be structurally bonded to a greater or lesser degree. According to Becker (1981), it can be distinguished by a greater or lesser accumulation of *marital-specific capital,* but nevertheless marriage and LAT relationships start out from different *baselines* or different *levels of organization* (Borell, 2001). Just like marriage, LAT relationships are based on mutual love and attraction, and in addition the partners develop various moral commitments to one another. However, LAT relationships have few, if any, of the structural foundations upon which marriage rests. As this study of LAT relationships of older people shows, the partners have virtually no common ownership of resources. Their private economies are quite separate and they have a very limited degree of shared possessions or savings (moreover, there is no indication that joint ownership tends to increase over the years, which would make LAT relationships more "marriage-like"). Furthermore, older LAT partners do not usually have children in common and neither do they have a shared extended family network that binds them together. In addition, LAT relationships have a low degree of institutionalization, that is, there are no legal bonds between the partners and there are few clear cultural conventions or established patterns of behavior that the partners can fall back on. In many if not in all of these circumstances, the multi-household organization of the relationship plays a crucial role. Establishing a multi-household LAT relationship, as opposed to living under the same roof, places radically different demands on the need for coordination of time, action, and resources.

In consequence of this, the bond between LAT partners is principally about mutual emotional and moral commitment. The focus of the relationship is on the intimacy itself and on the giving and receiving of chiefly emotional support. Thereby, it depends fundamentally on the mutual satisfaction generic to the relationship, rather than on structural bonds.

Ageing, Gender, and LAT Relationships

LAT relationships can offer older divorcees, widows, and widowers a fulfilling intimate relationship, but they can also ensure the individual a significant degree of autonomy. As this study has clearly shown, autonomy is of particular importance to women. They want to have an intimate relationship, but still have time for their daily choice of activities. Above all they are not prepared to accept a gendered division of labor in return for intimacy. This does not mean that the new LAT relationships lack mutual commitments, but these commitments would seem to deal less with traditional gender-based demands of personal service within marriage, and more with the giving and receiving of emotional support (and a limited instrumental support when necessary, for example, if one of the partners falls ill).

This balance is achieved through the partners retaining a home of their own. For women in LAT relationships a home of their own is a place in which personal control is ensured and optimized; a resource which they draw on to balance their need for privacy with their need for intimacy. Thus, even if the division of labor between men and women in LAT relationships is relatively traditional when they are together, their own home represents a central boundary-setting resource: *"His home is his, and my home is mine."*

The instrumental role older women seem to play in the formation of LAT relationships is not coincidental. The history of the older women who are active in the everyday experimentation of finding new forms of intimacy is, to a great extent, the history of a cohort who have been pioneers of the restructuring of family life in the past thirty to forty years. The women in today's LAT relationships experienced, when still quite young, a unique period of history, the 1950s, when the ideal of the nuclear family became more generally widespread, that is, a dominant ideal characterized by a distinct segregation of public and domestic spheres. Here the household, or rather, in this context, the *home*, was identified as primarily a female sphere:

the mother and wife was the heart of the home, and caring and household chores were female tasks.

Equally they belong to the cohort of women who gradually participated in a massive shift from unpaid work to wage labor. The altered position of women in the public sphere did not, however, bring with it an equivalent change in the domestic sphere. Instead, women had to take on a "second shift" of housework and childcare (Hochschild, 1989). During a period stretching from the 1960s onwards, the number of divorces increased dramatically in almost the entire Western world. This can be seen as the first indication of strains arising in a largely unaltered family model which was ill-adapted to women's increasing participation in paid work outside the home. Women not only initiated divorces to a greater extent than men, but they were also instrumental in efforts to create more autonomous and equal relationships, both inside and outside the framework of marriage (see, for example, Crosbie-Burnett and Giles-Sims, 1991). The everyday experimentation by older Swedish women with LAT relationships can be seen as an extension of this goal, *as the gender revolution continuing into old age*. If their previous marital households represented a constitutive force in the reproduction of traditional gendered relations, their own household today constitutes a resource base from which they may avoid an asymmetrical distribution of household labor and unequal demands of caring for a partner.

However, it would probably be premature to interpret LAT relationships as the product of an exclusively female strategy or interest. It is reasonable to at least speculate about the connection between the inherent qualities of LAT relationships, suggested in this study, and the psychological processes of ageing.

Social gerontologists from a variety of approaches have in recent years drawn attention to the fact that although older people often tend to avoid superfluous social interaction, they seem to value the emotional side of social relationships more than younger adults (Carstensen, 1992). Moreover, the quality of their social interaction is more important for positive life adjustment than frequency of contact (Fisher et al., 1989). LAT relationships, as opposed to other types of relationship that presuppose cohabitation, are well suited to the gradual change in values that is typical of older people. In LAT-relationships the emotional content of the relationship is brought into focus and, in contrast to marriage, there is no automatic development of increasing commitments and responsibilities implied in the relationship.

References

Ahron, C. R., and Rodgers, R. H. (1987). *Divorced families: A multidisciplinary developmental view.* New York: W. W. Norton and Company.

Allen, R., Blieszner, R., and Roberto, K. A. (2000). Families in the middle and later years: A review and critique of research in the 1990s. *Journal of Marriage and the Family,* 62, 911–926.

Becker, G. (1960). Notes on the concept of commitment. *American Journal of Sociology,* 66, 32–40.

Becker, G. (1981). *A treatise on the family.* Cambridge, MA: Harvard University Press.

Blomberg, S., Edebalk, P. G., and Petersson, J. (2000). The withdrawal of the welfare state: Elderly care in Sweden in the 1990s. *Nutritional Neuroscience,* 3, 151–153.

Borell, K. (2001). I stället för äktenskap: Åldrande och nya intimitetsformer. [Instead of marriage: Aging and new forms of intimacy.] *Gerontologia,* 15, 147–156.

Borell, K., and Ghazanfareeon Karlsson, S. (2000). Ældre kærestefolk – hvert sit hjem. [Living apart together in old age.] *Gerontologi og Samfund,* 16, 85–87.

Burch, T. K. (1990). Remarriage of older Canadians: Description and interpretation. *Research on Aging,* 12, 546–559.

Brubaker, T. H. (1990). Families in later life: A burgeoning research area. *Journal of Marriage and the Family,* 52, 959–981.

Bulcroft, K. A., and O'Connor, M. (1986). The importance of dating relationships on quality of life for older persons. *Family Relations,* 35, 397–401.

Bulcroft, R. A., and Bulcroft, K. A. (1991). The nature and functions of dating in later life. *Research on Aging,* 13, 244–260.

Carstensen, L. (1992). Social and Emotional patterns in adulthood: Support for socioemotional selectivity theory. *Psychology and Aging,* 7, 331-338.

Cherlin, A. J. (1999). *Public and private families: An introduction.* Second ed. Boston: McGraw-Hill.

Cherlin, A. J., and Furstenberg, F. (1986). *The new American grandparent: A place in the family, a life apart.* New York: Basic Books.

Crosbie-Burnett, M., and Giles-Sims, J. (1991). Marital power in stepfather families: A test of normative resource theory. *Journal of Family Psychology,* 4, 484–496.

Fisher, C. B., Reid, J. D., and Melendez, M. (1989). Conflict in families and friendship of later life. *Family Relations,* 38, 83–89.

Goldscheider, F. K. (1990). The aging of the gender revolution: What do we know and what do we need to know? *Research on Aging,* 12, 531–545.

Hadenius, S., and Weibull, L. (2000). *Massmedier: en bok om press, radio och TV.* [Mass media: A book about press, radio and TV.] Stockholm: Bonnier.

Hochschild, A. (1989). *The second shift: Working parents and the revolutions at home.* New York: Viking.

Johnson, M. E. (1991). Commitment to personal relationships. In W. H. Jones and D. Perlman (Eds.), *Advances in Personal Relationships* (Vol. III, pp. 117–143). London: Jessica Kingsley.

Johnson, M. P., and Caughlin, J. P. (1999). The tripartite nature of marital commitment: personal, moral, and structural reasons to stay married. *Journal of Marriage and Family,* 61, 160–178.

Kaplan, L. (2001). A couplehood typology for spouses of institutionalized persons with Alzheimer's Disease: Perception of "We" – "I". *Family Relations,* 50, 87–98.

Lee, R. M. (1993). *Doing research on sensitive topics*. London: Sage.
Levin, I., and Trost, J. (1999). Living apart together. *Community, Work and Family*, 2, 279–294.
Lopata, H. Z. (1996). *Current widowhood: Myths and realities*. Thousand Oaks: Sage.
Maccoby, E. E., and Mnookin, R. H. (1992). *Dividing the child: Social and legal dilemmas of custody*. Cambridge, MA: Harvard University Press.
Steitz, J. A., and Welker, K. G. (1990). Remarriage in later life: A critique and review of the literature. *Journal of Women and Aging*, 2, 81–90.
Swedish Central Bureau of Statistics, (1968–2000). *Befolkningsstatistik*. [Population statistics.] Stockholm: Statistics Sweden.
Swedish Central Bureau of Statistics, (1992a). *Population and housing census 1990. Part 2: Population and cohabitation*. Stockholm: Statistics Sweden.
Swedish Central Bureau of Statistics, (1992b). *Befolkning och utbildning*. [Population and education.] Stockholm: Statistics Sweden.
Swedish Central Bureau of Statistics, (1992c). *Befolkning och hälsa*. [Population and health.] Stockholm: Statistics Sweden.
Swedish National Board of Health and Welfare. (2000). *Äldreuppdraget: Slutrapport*. [Old age care: Final report.] Stockholm: Socialstyrelsen.
Talbott, M. M. (1998). Older widow's attitudes towards men and remarriage. *Journal of Ageing Studies*, 12, 429–450.
Weston, K. (1991). *Families we choose: Lesbians, gays, kinship*. New York: Colombia University Press.
Wilson, G. (1995). I'm the eyes and she's the arms: Changes in gender roles in advanced old age. In: S. Arber and J. Ginn (Eds.), *Connecting gender and ageing: A sociological approach* (pp. 98–113). Buckingham: Open University Press.
Winfield, F. E. (1985). *Commuter marriage: Living together, apart*. New York: Colombia University Press.

2

Late-Life Widowhood in the United States: New Directions in Research and Theory

Deborah Carr and Rebecca Utz

Widowhood is considered the most distressing and life-altering transition experienced by older adults (Holmes and Rahe, 1967). Yet the meaning and personal consequences of spousal loss are contingent on the larger social and historical context. In the United States, where the modern nuclear family is socially and economically autonomous, spouses may have few alternative sources of social, emotional, or instrumental support (Lopata, 1973; Volkart and Michael, 1957). When one's spouse dies, the survivor must adjust psychologically to the loss of their closest confidante, and must manage the daily decisions and responsibilities that were once shared by both spouses (Carey, 1979-1980; Umberson et al., 1992). The adjustments required by widowed spouses may be particularly difficult in societies which maintain a rigid gender-based allocation of social roles; men and women may have little experience in fulfilling the instrumental and expressive roles previously performed by their spouses.

The meaning and personal consequences of widowhood also are embedded in the larger demographic and technological context. In the United States today, adults are living longer than ever before, and chronically ill adults increasingly have access to life-sustaining technologies and treatments (Field and Cassel, 1997). The event of spousal death now typically occurs very late in life, but the process of becoming widowed may begin years prior to the actual death, starting with the onset of the spouse's chronic illness. Aspects of the dying process, including how, where, and when one's spouse dies may have profound implications for how the elderly bereaved person adjusts to the loss.

Although the death of a spouse is envisioned as the most private and personal of life transitions, we argue that the psychological and social consequences of spousal loss are inextricably linked to prevailing macrosocial conditions, such as cause of death structure and gender-based allocation of social roles in and outside the home; dyadic characteristics, including the quality of the marital relationship; and individual-level attributes, such as gender and personality of both the deceased spouse and survivor. We further propose that late-life widowhood is best conceptualized as a multifaceted process that may occur over a prolonged time period, rather than a dichotomous event that occurs upon the exact moment of a spouse's death. Further, we suggest that bereavement researchers should focus on a broad array of psychological, social, and behavioral outcomes in order to best develop interventions to improve the quality of life for older widowed persons.

In this chapter, we briefly review several methodological and theoretical challenges facing researchers studying late-life widowhood. We then provide an overview of new research findings from the Changing Lives of Older Couples (CLOC)[1] study, a prospective study of older widowed persons and matched controls in the United States. Specifically, we summarize research on: (1) the implications of late-life longevity for bereaved spouses; (2) marital quality and its consequences for spousal grief; (3) social and daily-life adjustments to late-life bereavement; and (4) "special event" grief. Taken together, this research highlights the ways in which the widowhood transition is molded by macrosocial conditions, dyadic characteristics, and individual-level attributes of the deceased and the survivor. Finally, we discuss the implications of our findings for policy, practice, and research on future cohorts of bereaved elders.

Challenges in Studying Late-life Bereavement

Despite widespread belief that widowhood is among the most stressful of life events (Holmes and Rahe, 1967), most studies find that only 15 to 30 percent of survivors experience clinically significant depression in the year following their spouse's death (Jacobs et al., 1989; Lund et al., 1985-86; Stroebe et al., 1993; Zisook and

Shuchter, 1991). Less severe psychological reactions are more common. Depending on the sample and assessment procedure used, roughly 40 to 70 percent of widowed persons experience dysphoria, or a period of two or more weeks marked by feelings of sadness, immediately after the loss (e.g., Bruce et al., 1990; Zisook et al., 1997).

At first glance, these statistics suggest that depression and distress are typical reactions to loss, but on closer inspection they also reveal the remarkable psychological resilience of the widowed; at least 70 to 80 percent experience the widowhood transition without clinical depression, while roughly half survive spousal loss without a two-week spell of low mood. Thus, widowhood researchers face the challenge of identifying those characteristics of the bereaved, their spouses, the marital relationship, and the death process that protect against decrements in psychological well-being.

Methodological Issues

Past research also reveals stark inconsistencies in the strength of the relationship between widowhood and psychological distress (e.g., Stroebe et al., 1993; Wortman and Silver, 1989; Zisook et al., 1997). We propose at least five methodological reasons for the inconclusiveness of past research. First, many studies of widowhood are based on samples of the widowed only, thus it is impossible directly to ascertain the effect of the widowhood transition. For instance, studies of depression rates among samples of the bereaved only cannot ascertain whether these rates are higher, lower, or the same as those found among non-bereaved peers. Second, most research is based on cross-sectional, or one-time snapshot data. Thus, it is not possible to control for those pre-loss characteristics that affect both one's risk of widowhood, and one's reactions to the widowhood transition. The deleterious psychological effects of spousal loss may be overstated if pre-loss characteristics that elevate the risk of both widowhood and depression, such as poverty or poor health, are not controlled. Third, the psychological, social, and economic consequences of widowhood may attenuate over time, thus studies which focus on relatively long time horizons may underestimate the short-term consequences. Moreover, studies that do not control the duration since death may yield inconclusive findings (Bruce et al., 1990; Ferraro, 1984; Futterman et al., 1990; Lund et al., 1989; Mendes de Leon et al., 1994).

Fourth, different aspects of psychological and social adjustment may follow different trajectories and may be affected by different aspects of the widowhood process (Jacobs et al., 1987-88). Consequently, analyses that focus only on broad outcomes, such as overall grief, depression, or social participation across all domains, may mask patterns among more specific symptoms and outcomes. Fifth, many studies of spousal loss are based on samples spanning a broad age range, with little attention paid to age differences in how bereavement is experienced. Widowhood is a less "selective" phenomenon among older adults, for whom spousal death is a fairly normative and anticipated transition (Neugarten and Hagestad, 1976). Thus, the personal consequences of spousal loss may be less severe for older adults than for the young or midlife widowed. Finally, a guiding assumption of much bereavement research is that widowhood is a monolithic event that can be captured with a simple dichotomous variable. We argue that the transition to widowhood can occur in many different ways, and that the conditions under which an individual makes the transition to widowhood may have important ramifications for their post-loss psychological and social well-being.

The Changing Lives of Older Couples (CLOC) Study

Sample Characteristics

Many new and previously unresolved questions about late-life widowhood can be addressed with the CLOC study, a large multiwave prospective study of spousal bereavement. This study is based on a two-stage area probability sample of 1,532 married men and women from the Detroit (Michigan) Standardized Metropolitan Statistical Area (SMSA). To be eligible for the study, respondents had to be English-speaking members of a married couple in which the husband was age sixty-five or older. All sample members were non-institutionalized and were capable of participating in a two-hour face-to-face interview. The response rate for the baseline interview was 68 percent, which is consistent with the response rate from other Detroit area studies in that period.

Baseline face-to-face interviews with the married older adults were conducted from June 1987 through April 1988. Spousal loss was subsequently monitored using monthly death record tapes provided by the State of Michigan and by reading the daily obituaries in Detroit-area newspapers. The National Death Index (NDI) and direct ascertainment of death certificates were used to confirm deaths and obtain causes of death. Of the 335 persons known to have lost a spouse during the study period, 316 were contacted for possible interview (19 persons, or 6 percent had died during the interim). Of the 316 contacted, 263 persons (83 percent) participated in at least one of the three follow-up interviews which were conducted six months (Wave 1), 18 months (Wave 2), and 48 months (Wave 3) after the spouse's death. Each widowed person was assigned a same-age, same-sex non-bereaved matched control from the baseline sample, and this control was also interviewed at each of the three follow-ups.

All analyses presented here use weighted data, which adjusts for unequal probabilities of selection and differential response rate at baseline. Most analyses presented in this paper are based on the 211 widowed persons (59 men and 152 women) and the 87 matched controls (22 men and 65 women) who were interviewed at the six-month follow up. Several analyses also evaluate the longer-term consequence of loss, and focus on the 178 widowed persons (51 men and 127 women) and 202 matched controls (58 men and 144 women) who were interviewed at the 18-month follow up.[2]

Strengths of the CLOC Study

The CLOC study has several desirable properties that make it an ideal data set for studying the consequences of late-life widowhood. First, the sample includes both men and women, thus it is possible to explore gender differences in the experience of widowhood. Second, all interviews with widowed persons (and matched controls) were conducted exactly six, eighteen, and forty-eight months following the death, thus all analyses "hold constant" the duration of time that has passed since the loss. Third, because the data are prospective and include rich information on the widowed persons, their spouses, and their marital relationship prior to the loss, we are able to prospectively study changes in psychological and social well-being after the loss. Moreover, we can control those factors that increase one's risk of (or "selection" into) widowhood and that affect adjustment to widowhood. Fourth, all widowed persons are assigned a same-age and same-sex "matched control" from the baseline sample, thus the true effects of widowhood can be differentiated from those related to aging or the passage of time.

Finally, the CLOC study includes rich data on both global aspects of psychological and social adjustment, such as depression and anxiety, as well as specific loss-related outcomes, such as yearning and grief. Specific symptoms and behaviors may respond in very different ways to different aspects of the widowhood transition, and these (potentially) competing effects may cancel out one another when only an aggregated scale is used as an outcome variable. For instance, widely used grief scales such as the Bereavement Index (Jacobs et al., 1986), Present Feelings About Loss (Singh and Raphael, 1981), and Texas Revised Inventory of Grief (Zisook et al., 1982) typically include several symptom subscales, such as anger or yearning (see table 2.1). These subscales respond differently to different aspects of spousal loss, thus the use of an overarching grief scale only may conceal patterns among specific symptoms.

Table 2.1

Summary of Items That Contribute to the Grief Scale and Subscales, Changing Lives of Older Couples Study, 1987-1993

Anxiety (a = .71)	Afraid of what is ahead Felt anxious or unsettled Worried about how you would manage your day to day affairs
Despair (a = .64)	Life seemed empty Felt empty inside Felt life had lost its meaning
Shock (a = .77)	Felt in a state of shock Couldn't believe what was happening Felt emotionally numb
Anger (a = .68)	Felt resentful or bitter about death Felt death was unfair Felt anger towards God
Yearning (a = .75)	Longing to have him/her with you Painful waves of missing him/her Feelings of intense pain and grief Feelings of grief or lonliness
Intrusive Thoughts (a = .66)	Difficulty falling asleep, thoughts of him/her kept coming into your mind Tried to block out memories or thoughts of him/her Couldn't get thoughts of him/her out of my head
Grief (a = .88)	[All 19 items above]

Note: All items referred to the month prior to interview and were coded on a 4-point scale: 1= No, never, 2= Yes, but rarely, 3= Yes, sometimes, 4= Yes, often

Recent Findings from the CLOC

We now provide an overview of findings from recent empirical research based on the CLOC study. Specifically, we present findings on: (1) the implications of late-life longevity for bereaved spouses; (2) marital quality and its consequences for spousal grief; (3) social and daily-life adjustments to late-life bereavement; and (4) "special event" grief. We will summarize the research findings, highlight the importance of our findings for policy and practice, and discuss the implications of our research for understanding the widowhood experience among future cohorts of older adults. Taken together, these research projects underscore the importance of the three theoretical considerations outlined earlier in the paper, that: the experience and consequences of widowhood are molded by macrosocial conditions, dyadic characteristics, and individual-level attributes; widowhood is multifaceted process—not a dichotomous event; and responses to widowhood comprise a diverse array of psychological, social, and behavioral adjustments.

Late-Life Longevity and its Implications for Bereaved Spouses

Late-Life Death in the United States. One of the most important demographic shifts in the United States over the past century is the extraordinary gain in life expectancy experienced by older adults. In 1900, a newborn could expect to live until age forty-seven. Persons who survived until age sixty-five in 1900 could expect to live another 11.9 years (Guralnik et al., 1996). In stark contrast, life expectancy at birth currently tops seventy-five years, and sixty-five year olds can expect to survive another 17.5 years (National Center for Health Statistics, 1992). This precipitous increase in life expectancy is due, in part, to a shift in the nature and causes of death over the past century. While acute and infectious diseases of infancy and childhood were the leading causes of death at the beginning of the twentieth century, the leading causes of death today are chronic diseases, or ongoing conditions that may add years of discomfort, disability, and dependence to the aging patient's life. Heart disease, stroke, and cancer are now the leading causes of death, and these three illnesses account for 67 percent of all deaths to older adults in the United States (Rosenberg et al., 1996: 31). An implication of these demographic patterns is that late-life widowhood is increasingly experienced as the endpoint of a prolonged and often painful dying process, rather than an acute event that happens suddenly and unexpectedly. Scientific, medical, and public health advances throughout the twentieth century arguably have made "living easier and dying harder" (Field and Cassel 1997).

Is dying also harder for widowed persons whose spouse's deaths occur slowly and painfully? The CLOC research team investigated: (1) whether older widowed persons adjust better psychologically to sudden, unexpected deaths or anticipated deaths that occur following a long illness period; and (2) whether other characteristics of the spouse's dying trajectory affect the survivor's psychological adjustment to loss (Carr, 2003; Carr et al., 2001).

Coping with Sudden Versus Expected Spousal Deaths. Are gradual and anticipated deaths, or sudden, unexpected deaths more difficult to cope with? Some studies suggest that sudden spousal death is associated with poorer psychological adjustment among the widowed, because the married couple did not have the opportunity to resolve emotional, financial, and practical "unfinished business" (e.g., Blauner, 1966; Jacobs et al., 1986; O'Bryant, 1990-91). Other studies find that anticipated deaths are linked to poorer adjustment among the widowed (e.g., Gerber, 1974; Sanders, 1982-83), while others still find no relationship between death expectedness and survivors' psychological adjustment (e.g., Hill, Thompson, and Gallagher, 1988; Roach and Kitson, 1989).

These conflicting findings are due largely to the fact that important aspects of the dying process which are correlated with death expectedness were not controlled in past studies. Consequently, the actual effects of death expectedness may be either counteracted or suppressed by omitted variables. For instance, the forewarning period may be punctuated by potentially distressing experiences such as difficult caregiving duties (Anashensel et al., 1997), financial strains imposed by costly medical and long-term care (Field and Cassel, 1997; Warshawsky, 2000), emotional isolation from family members and friends (Kramer, 1996-97), and the neglect of one's own health (Rosenblatt, 1983; Sanders, 1982-83; Siegel and Weinstein, 1983; Sweeting and Gilhooly, 1990). Yet other experiences that accompany a slow death process may be associated with better spousal adjustment following the loss (O'Bryant, 1990-91). Couples who anticipate a death may have the opportunity to resolve "unfinished business" and to make practical plans for the survivor's economic and social adjustment, thus enabling a smoother transition to widowhood (Blauner, 1966; Rando, 1986).

Our analysis explores the effects of death suddenness and expectedness on the surviving spouse's psychological adjustment in both the short- and longer-term (i.e., six and eighteen months following the loss). We adjust for important indicators of the death context, including spouse's age at death, whether the respondent was providing care to his/her spouse in the six months prior to the death, whether the spouse was residing in a nursing home prior to death, whether the couple talked about the impending death, and whether the survivor was with their dying spouse at the moment of death. These indicators capture both positive aspects of the forewarning period, such as discussions and closure-seeking, as well as negative aspects, including caregiving strain.

Regression models were used to evaluate the effects of death forewarning and death context on diverse aspects of the bereaved spouse's psychological adjustment, and all models controlled demographic, socioeconomic, health, and pre-loss characteristics. The analyses revealed that some grief symptoms are heightened by sudden deaths, while other symptoms are exacerbated by anticipated deaths. However, these competing effects would have cancelled out each other and gone undetected if we had used only a broad grief scale which agglomerates diverse symptoms. Widowed persons whose spouses died suddenly had more frequent intrusive thoughts six months after the loss, although this effect faded by the eighteen-month follow up. This finding is consistent with research examining symptoms of post-traumatic stress disorder among the bereaved. In the short-term, unprovoked thoughts of the deceased and the sudden death haunt the survivor, yet these thoughts fade over time as the widowed person becomes enmeshed in other activities and relationships (Parkes, 1985; Parkes and Brown, 1972).

In contrast, deaths that occur after more than six months of forewarning are associated with elevated anxiety levels at both six and eighteen months after the death. Persons who spend more time awaiting their spouse's impending death are presumably at a greater risk of experiencing concurrent stressors than those whose anticipation periods are confined to a shorter time frame. It is also possible that the elderly spouses who died slowly suffered cognitive impairment during their final stages, thus preventing the couple from engaging in meaningful conversation and preparation for death.

These findings underscore the importance of conceptualizing widowhood as a process that may begin far earlier than the actual moment of death, and which extends well beyond the initial mourning period. Interventions targeted toward older adults providing care to their ailing spouse may be as important for alleviating bereavement-related anxiety as interventions offered to the newly bereaved. Future research should explore how combinations of forewarning time and precise causes of death, such as Alzheimer's disease, condition the effect of loss on survivors' psychological adjustment. As our research has demonstrated, how the dying patient and his/her spouse experience the final months of life has profound implications for the psychological adjustment of the survivor.

Our research also reveals that men and women experience the process of spousal death very differently. For women, sudden deaths are associated with elevated yearning for one's spouse. Men, in contrast, yearn most for their deceased wives when they died after a prolonged illness. Given gendered patterns of socialization and social interaction in the United States, men typically have fewer sources of friendship and social support over the life course than do women (Antonucci, 1990). During the final stages of his wife's life, a man may become even more emotionally bonded to his spouse, at the expense of his already few and tenuous relationships with others. Moreover, given gender differences in mortality, men may have few same-sex peers who are caring for a dying spouse, and thus few sources of guidance and support. In contrast, women may rely on their female friends' direct experience with spousal illness to prepare them for the difficult dying process and thereafter (Fooken, 1985). Peer education or peer-counseling programs targeted to male care givers and widowers may be a particularly effective strategy for assisting men whose wives are dying slowly from terminal illness.

A "Good Death" For Whom? Spousal Death Quality and Survivor's Psychological Adjustment. In the United States, policy makers, scholars and practitioners share the concern that advanced medical technologies have made "living easier and dying harder" (Field and Cassel, 1997). This widespread concern—that the sick and dying can prolong the length, though not necessarily the quality, of their lives—was a driving force behind the passage of the 1990 Patient Self-Determination Act and a growing Hospice movement. Both seek to give the dying and their families the opportunity actively to manage the death process; the guiding assumption is that if the dying patient and family decide when, how, and under what conditions death occurs, then the process of dying will be less distressing both to the patient and surviving kin. However, we know of no empirical studies that have evaluated directly whether characteristics of the death, such as how much pain the deceased was subject to, the location of the death, and the psychological state of the dying patient affect the surviving spouse's adjustment to loss.

Carr (2003) examined whether the psychological adjustment of elderly widowed persons six months following spousal death is affected by the nature of their spouse's dying experience. Based on theoretical and philosophical writings on "dying well" and the "good death" (e.g., Byock, 1996; Field and Cassel, 1997; Webb, 1997), five aspects of death quality were considered: the patient's acceptance of their impending death, social support from loved ones, degree of burden on others, death timeliness, and appropriate physical care. Each of these indicators characterized the dying experience of the now-deceased spouse, and was based on the surviving spouse's retrospective report obtained six months following the death. A diverse array of psychological outcomes (including depression, anxiety, grief, and specific grief symptoms) were regressed on each of the death quality indicators, and demographic, socioeconomic status, and pre-loss characteristics were controlled. Objective characteristics of the death, including the cause of death and duration of the illness, also were adjusted in all models.

Despite widespread belief in the clinical and religious community that a "good death" may ease psychological adjustment for widowed persons (e.g., Byock, 1996; Webb, 1997), we found only partial empirical support for the proposed linkages between death quality and survivor adjustment. Two dimensions of "death quality": the dying spouse's acceptance of his/her impending death, and the surviving spouse's belief that the deceased had led a full life, did not predict survivor's psychological adjustment. Rather, survivors' psychological adjustment was most closely linked to physical aspects of the death. Widowed persons reporting that their spouse had considerable physical pain prior to death report significantly higher levels of yearning for their deceased spouse, significantly elevated post-loss anxiety and anger levels, and significantly more intrusive thoughts. Those whose spouses died due to physician or hospital negligence evidenced significantly higher levels of anger. Anger is considered a particularly difficult symptom of loss, because it is linked to social isolation and rejection of social support from friends and family. Again, these important symptom-specific patterns would have been masked had we considered only a broad outcome measure, such as overall grief.

One aspect of the dying process presumed to be undesirable for the dying patient actually proved protective to survivors. The surviving spouses of those who lived in nursing homes at the end of life showed less anxiety than the survivors of those who were living at home. Placing one's husband or wife in a nursing home may psychologically prepare spouses for the permanent separation of widowhood, and may spare them from the strains of providing direct care. Taken together, these findings suggest that improved medical care, affordable nursing home, long-term, or hospice care, and increased availability of pain management programs will not only benefit the dying person, but may also enable a smoother transition to widowhood among their surviving spouses.

Late-Life Grief: A Function of Marital Quality and Spouse's Personality?

Marital Quality and Spousal Bereavement. How older adults experience widowhood is inextricably linked to how they experienced marriage. We propose that the degree to which the bereaved mourn the loss of their spouse may be commensurate with the psychological and social benefits received in the marriage; those with warm, trusting relationships may grieve more than those with conflicted marriages. However, early research—guided largely by the psychoanalytic tradition—suggests that widowed persons with the most troubled marriages suffer heightened (and delayed) grief following their spouse's death (Freud, 1917/1957). This perspective holds that survivors who had strained or conflicted marital relationships find it hard to let go of their spouses, yet they also feel angry at the deceased for abandoning them and thus experience elevated depression. Empirical support for this hypothesis is undermined by a serious methodological limitation; most studies measure marital quality retrospectively after the spouse's death, and thus widowed persons' characterizations of their marriages are often shaped by their current emotional state (e.g., Parkes and Weiss, 1983). Persons who are most depressed after the loss may offer the most negative retrospective accounts of their marriages (Bonnano et al., 1998) because depressed individuals evaluate themselves, their relationships, and their past experiences more negatively than do nondepressed persons (Abramson et al., 1978; Beck, 1967; Hirschfield et al., 1989; Teasdale et al., 1980). Yet bereaved people may also "sanctify"—or offer unrealistically positive evaluations of—their late spouse and marriage in retrospect (Lopata, 1973).

Research from the CLOC project explores whether pre-loss marital quality affects widowed persons' psychological adjustment following the loss (Carr et al., 2000). Our research reveals that the bereaved yearn most for their deceased spouses when the marital relationship was marked by closeness and interdependence. Persons in conflicted marriages reported significantly less yearning for their deceased spouses, thus calling into question earlier psychoanalytic-based assumptions about spousal bereavement (Carr et al., 2000). Troubled marriages appear to diminish, rather than exacerbate, grief and mourning.

Are All Deceased Spouses Missed? The degree to which widowed elders are grief-stricken is also linked to personality characteristics of their spouses; some spouses are "missed" more than others. The CLOC research team investigated whether the bereaved spouse's grief is associated with the deceased spouse's personality traits, measured at baseline (Sonnega, 2001a). Prior to their death, the now-deceased spouses completed the NEO Five-Factor Personality Inventory (Costa and McCrae, 1985), which measures five personality dimensions: agreeableness (the inclination toward interpersonal trust and consideration of others); conscientiousness (the tendency toward persistence, industriousness, and organization); extraversion (the disposition toward positive emotion); neuroticism (the tendency to experience emotional distress), and openness (a receptive orientation toward varied experiences and ideas). Spouses who had a deep appreciation for art and beauty (i.e., the aesthetics subscale of the openness to experience scale) were not grieved for as much as those who did not show these characteristics. In contrast, persons with conscientious spouses had a much lower risk of major depressive disorder following the loss, suggesting that the transition to widowhood may be easier in terms of death-related stressors, such as financial and legal matters, when one's spouse was well organized and hard working.

Our findings clearly reveal that not all losses are equal. Although widowhood historically has been viewed as an event that inevitably and universally triggers grief and sorrow (see Archer, 1999 for review), our research shows instead that the emotional consequences of bereavement are contingent upon how rewarding or conflicted the marital relationship was prior to loss. Moreover, individual-level characteristics of the deceased, such as conscientiousness or a pleasant demeanor, may make some spouses "missed" more than others. Although some deaths may not actually trigger grief among the widowed, rigid normative expectations for the expression of emotion are often imposed on the bereaved (Averill, 1968). Widowed persons' failure to comply with normative expressions of grief, such as openly yearning for a deceased spouse, may be subtly sanctioned: a denial of grief may be interpreted as "a sign of actual or potential pathology" (Averill, 1968). By considering one's marital history prior to spousal death, variations in bereavement may be better understood.

Our findings also imply that emotional adjustment to spousal loss may become more difficult for future cohorts of older adults. The members of the CLOC sample, most of whom were born between 1900 and 1920, belong to a birth cohort who experienced very low levels of divorce, given both the social stigma accompanying divorce, and the scarcity of opportunities for women to provide for themselves economically in earlier decades (Cherlin, 1981; Holden and Smock, 1991). Thus, some men and women of the CLOC cohort may have remained in marriages that provided relatively low levels of warmth and relatively high levels of conflict. If current cohorts of young and midlife couples choose to dissolve dissatisfying marriages, then those who remain married until late life may have highly satisfying marriages and thus may suffer worse upon spousal death.

Social and Behavioral Adjustments to Spousal Loss

The death of a spouse represents more than the severing of an emotional attachment to one's partner and confidante (Bowlby, 1980). Widowhood also alters the routines, tasks, and living arrangements that characterized the everyday life of the married couple. The bereaved must reconstruct their daily lives to reflect their new status as an unmarried person; this process typically involves modifying the daily decisions, household tasks, and routine responsibilities that were once shared by both spouses (Carey, 1979-1980). Although a voluminous literature explores the mental and physical health consequences of widowhood (see Stroebe et al., 2001; Waite and Gallagher, 2000 for review), relatively little is known about the social and behavioral adjustments made by older bereaved spouses. Documenting the practical and "daily life" consequences of late-life spousal loss is critically important, and can help practitioners and scholars to develop a deeper understanding of the challenges faced by the widowed as they navigate their new (or newly reconfigured) social roles.

The CLOC research team explored the consequences of widowhood for three aspects of everyday life: informal and formal social participation; housework and household maintenance activities; and the exchange of emotional and financial support among bereaved spouses and their children (Ha et al., [in press]; Utz et al., 2002; Utz et al., [in press]). This research brings into sharp focus the ways that gender-based allocation of social roles inside and outside the home affects social and psychological adjustment among current cohorts of the bereaved elderly.

Social Participation Among the Bereaved Elderly. Utz, et al. (forthcoming) investigated whether and how widowhood affects older adults' participation in formal and informal social activities. Formal social activities include participation in clubs or organizations, while informal social activities include visits and conversations with friends and family. Widowhood is associated with increased levels of informal social participation, but not formal social participation. Upon closer inspection, we found that this increase in social contact is due largely to increased levels of social support offered to rather than sought by recently bereaved persons. Regardless of whether social support is actively sought or passively accepted, the majority of widowed persons named social activities and community involvement as strategies for coping with the stress and loneliness that often accompany widowhood. Although sustained social engagement appears to be a critical component of successful adaptation to widowhood, we caution practitioners against adopting a simple-minded "keep busy" edict when designing appropriate care and support strategies for the widowed. Rather than creating new recreational or social opportunities for the bereaved, intervention efforts should instead enable older adults' maintenance of their pre-loss social activities, interpersonal relationships, and hobbies—provided these activities are still deemed enjoyable and worthwhile by the newly bereaved.

Maintaining a Household After Spousal Death. The lives of the widowed also are altered in terms of their activities within the home:

the maintenance of their households remains a pressing concern for most older bereaved. The overwhelming majority of older married couples in the United States maintain their own household, separate from their children and extended family, up until the very last years of life. Roughly 95 percent of older adults live in their own independent residences, and 77 percent of older adults are homeowners (HUD, 1999). Consequently, when one spouse dies, the survivor is responsible for running the household and performing the tasks that were once performed by their spouse. The personal strain is often considerable, and is most acute for those who were highly dependent on their spouses prior to death. For instance, women in the CLOC study who were highly dependent on their spouses for household management tasks prior to loss evidenced significantly higher levels of post-death anxiety (Carr et al., 2000). In order to best develop interventions to assist the bereaved with their newly acquired daily responsibilities, researchers must obtain a fuller understanding of the nature of these responsibilities, and the alternative sources of support that the bereaved may have access to.

To this end, the CLOC research team examined how widowhood affects housework duties among elderly men and women, with a particular emphasis on the role that children and other family members play in helping the widowed to maintain their households (Utz et al., [in press]). Regression models were used to predict the amount of time an older person spends preparing meals and doing housework in an average week. The analyses revealed that widowhood decreases the amount of housework performed by women and increases the amount of housework done by men. This gender difference is due, in part, to the fact that adult children are more likely to assist their widowed mothers than their widowed fathers with household tasks following spousal loss.

Widowed mothers' dependence on their adult children for financial and legal advice also increases after the loss (Ha et al., [in press]). Both prior to and following spousal loss, women receive more instrumental support from their children than men do, and this support increases much more for women than men following the loss. However, the flows of intergenerational exchange are not solely upward to grieving parents: widowed women are more likely than men to give emotional support to their children following loss, reflecting gender-based patterns of parent-child closeness over the life course (ibid). Newly widowed mothers maintain their role as the family's emotional and expressive caretaker, even as they work through their own grief.

Gender-Based Social Roles: A Detriment to the Widowed? Given that marriages in the United States have traditionally adhered to a gender-based allocation of instrumental and expressive roles, it is not surprising that the loss of a spouse has quite different ramifications for widows and widowers. Our research also reveals the potentially harmful consequences of rigid adherence to gender-typed social roles. For men and women socialized to fulfill the "traditional" marriage contract, widowhood may represent the loss of a homemaker and confidante for men, and the loss of a decision maker and financial resource for women. The loss of a partner who performed highly specialized tasks in the home may create stress for the surviving spouse, if he or she lacks the skills to perform those tasks. Based on these findings, we urge practitioners to devise intervention programs that provide assistance with instrumental daily activities, if there is an unmet need due to the death of their spouse. One such strategy may be the development of support groups, where the bereaved can gain mastery over those tasks for which they lack skills, training, or prior experience (see Caserta et al., 1999 for example). Successful intervention programs should first identity precisely what is lost upon spousal death, and then fill the identified void.

We must caution that our findings may reflect the unique experiences of men and women born in the early twentieth century. For instance, current gender differences in mortality have created a highly imbalanced sex ratio among older Americans, where older women outnumber older men by 1.5 to 1 (United States Bureau of the Census, 1996). This imbalance could create a situation where older widowed men have a large pool of female helpmates to turn to, thus they may be less reliant on their children for instrumental and expressive support. Alternatively, current cohorts of older widowers may not need the same amount of informal support as do widows, due to early socialization experiences (Stevens, 1995). The development of personal attributes such as independence and self-reliance may have been imbued in young men, but not young women of the CLOC cohort.

Women of the CLOC cohort may have been socialized to rely on their husbands (when they were alive) and their children for household maintenance tasks, while their children may adhere to the stereotypical view that older women need more assistance and support than their presumably more capable male peers. Future generations of older women, who have higher levels of education, more years of paid work experience, and who participated in more egalitarian divisions of labor in their families (Bianchi, 1995), may be less susceptible to dependence on their husbands or children for tasks such as home repair and financial management. Yet in future generations, we may continue to witness adult children's tendency to provide support to their mothers, rather than their fathers. High rates of marital dissolution in the American family in the late twentieth century, coupled with a persistent division of labor which places primary responsibility for child rearing responsibility (and custody) in the hands of mothers, may create a context of weakened father-child relationships; such patterns may prove particularly harmful to future cohorts of widowed men, who may attempt to manage their lives without the support of wives or children.

Evaluating Clinical Wisdom: Anniversary Grief?

Just as spousal loss disrupts daily routines and activities, widowhood also alters the ways that older adults experience annual or periodic activities and celebrations. Mental health professionals and social scientists base important professional decisions on the assumption that the bereaved are likely to experience heightened grief on special occasions, such as wedding anniversaries, major holidays, and their deceased spouse's birthday. Special events are believed to trigger memories of the deceased spouse, and accompanying feelings of sadness, yearning, and grief (Rosenblatt, 1983). Psychological reactions to spousal loss may ebb and flow based on time and place; particular days and locations may elicit pleasant or painful memories of the deceased spouse.

The concept of "anniversary grief" has powerful ramifications for both research and practice. For instance, survey researchers typically interview widowed persons thirteen months (rather than twelve months) following their loss, for fear that an interview on the one-year anniversary of the loss may capture disproportionately high levels of dysphoric mood and disturbances in social functioning (Jacobs et al., 1987; Parkes and Weiss, 1983). Practitioners and authors of self-help literature regularly warn widowed individuals that they may experience recurrent grief at "special times . . . [including] holidays, anniversaries and birthdays" (University of Michigan Faculty and Staff Assistance Program, 2001: 21).

Despite the pervasive influence of the "anniversary grief" concept, we know of no research that has held this argument up to empirical scrutiny. Thus, the CLOC research team evaluated the hypothesis that widowed persons experience decrements in their emotional well-being upon special occasions (Sonnega, 2001b). Specifically, our research examined whether widowed elders experience an elevated risk of a major depressive disorder, and heightened levels of depressed mood, anxiety, and grief symptoms during the following time periods: (1) at or around the time of the deceased spouse's birthday; (2) during the month of January, believed to be a period of post-holiday blues, and (3) during the month of June, a time when the married couple would have celebrated wedding anniversaries or other family-centered events such as school graduations or Father's Day celebrations. Ordinary least squares regression models were estimated to evaluate whether widowed persons interviewed in January, June, or within one month of their deceased spouse's birthday had significantly poorer psychological health. All statistical models controlled potential confounders and mediators of the relationship, including demographic, health, and socioeconomic characteristics of both the surviving and recently deceased spouse.

The analyses revealed that widowed persons interviewed in June report significantly higher levels of yearning, despair, and grief-related anger. They also are twelve times more likely to report a major depressive episode than those interviewed in other months. Persons interviewed in January also have a significantly greater risk of major depressive disorder and grief, and this effect is significantly greater for widowed persons than for members of the control sample. Thus, while older adults appear to experience the post-holiday "blues," widowed persons are particularly susceptible to this experience. Bereaved persons interviewed within one month of their spouse's birthday have significantly elevated levels of grief, anxiety, depression, shock, and despair. However, birthdays do not appear to trigger major depressive episodes. Rather, this time appears to be marked by symptoms of tension and nervousness, perhaps due to uneasiness about how to observe a deceased spouse's birthday. Importantly, all of the effects described thus far are short-lived; the psychological impact of special occasions is confined to the first year following the loss, and is no longer present at the eighteen-month follow up.

Our finding that psychological distress, grief, and depression among widowed persons spike in January, June, and near the decedent's birthday has important ramifications for both research and practice. First, special occasion reactions may be a significant source of variance in bereavement studies, and thus should be accounted for in statistical analyses. Widowed persons interviewed near special occasions may overstate their feelings of distress, thus reliable diagnostic criteria for complicated or pathological grief should incorporate the timing of the mental health assessment. Second, counselors and practitioners should devise individual treatment strategies, community interventions, or special programs for widowed persons during the winter holiday season, and during the busy, event-dense month of June (Watson, 1994). A careful examination of death anniversary reactions may provide useful clinical observations about whether psychiatric complications have arisen in bereavement (Jacobs et al., 1987). Future research should examine whether special occasion grief reactions are indicative of a better or worse course of recovery.

Summary and Implications for Future Research

We have presented recent research findings from the Changing Lives of Older Couples study, and have highlighted the methodological, theoretical, and practical importance of this research. First, we identified a number of important methodological issues that scholars of late-life widowhood must take into consideration in order to develop a rich and empirically sound portrait of bereavement. The use of prospective, multiwave data that obtains information on both men and women, and on both widowed persons and non-bereaved controls is essential. Moreover, pre-loss data on both husbands' and wives' physical, emotional, economic, and social well-being is necessary if researchers hope to identify changes in well-being before and after the widowhood transition. Finally, researchers should move away from conceptualizing and operationalizing widowhood as a dichotomous event, and should develop theoretical and statistical models that capture the multifaceted nature of the widowhood process.

We also proposed that scholars and practitioners could obtain a richer and more accurate understanding of late-life widowhood by conceptualizing the process and consequences of widowhood as deeply embedded in the macrosocial and historical context, and as closely linked to characteristics of the marital dyad and individual-level characteristics of husband and wife.

Macrosocial Issues: Mortality and Morbidity in the United States

Our research has revealed that both how one's spouse dies, and the extent to which the dying process produces strain both before and after the actual death is closely linked to technological and demographic forces. Older widowed persons today are much more likely than prior generations to experience spousal loss as a slow and gradual process, beginning with the diagnosis of terminal illness, through the difficult stages of caregiving and care seeking, up until the eventual death (Field and Cassel, 1997). The dying process has critical implications for survivor well-being. Slow and expected deaths bring elevated anxiety to the surviving spouse in both the short- and longer-term (i.e., six and 18 months following loss), perhaps due to the fact that caregiving strain, cognitive decline on the part of one's spouse, and the potential for co-occurring stressors may outstrip the healthy spouse's ability to cope. Deaths marked by physical pain, and which were due, in part, to physician or hospital negligence are particularly difficult for bereaved spouses. Future health care policy, including legislation regarding end-of-life care, and funding for Hospice and palliative care, may have important implications for the well-being of the bereaved as well as the dying.

Dyadic Characteristics: The Implications of Marital Quality for the Bereaved

The psychological consequences of spousal loss are also contingent upon the quality and dynamics of one's marriage. Our research has shown that widowed persons whose marriages were marked by high levels of warmth and interdependence evidenced heightened levels of yearning following their loss, while conflicted and strained marriages led to significantly lower levels of yearning for one's spouse. Widowhood research that presumes that all marriages are created equal might have found that the effects of widowhood on yearning were either weak or non-significant; only when the quality of marriage is ascertained do we start to obtain a more accurate picture of how spousal loss affects psychological adjustment.

Individual-Level Characteristics: The Place of Gender in Bereavement Research

Individual-level characteristics are important moderators of the relationship between widowhood and survivor adjustment. Among the most important of these is gender. Emotional responses to loss vary by gender; for men, watching their wife die slowly is associated with elevated yearning, while for women, their husband's sudden and unanticipated death leads to heightened yearning. Behavioral responses vary as well; following spousal loss, women perform less housework and men perform more housework, largely because children come forward to provide instrumental support, and financial advice to their widowed mothers (but not fathers). Yet widowed women also are the providers of support; they are significantly more likely than widowed men to provide emotional support to their children upon the death of their father. Women's social embeddedness and relationships with their children may protect against the longer-term physical and emotional strains associated with spousal loss and with aging, more generally. In sum, our research revealed a number of important gender differences in how widowhood is experienced, and these differences reflect macrosocial patterns of gender role socialization over the life course, and gender-based allocation of social roles in and outside the home.

Bereavement among the Baby Boomers: Speculations from the CLOC Study

We caution that many of the findings documented in the CLOC study may be specific to men and women who were born in the early twentieth century, who went on to hold clearly demarcated gender roles in the family, and who experienced very low rates of marital dissolution (see Bianchi, 1995 for review). The experiences of future cohorts of bereaved elders may be quite different, given the rapid changes in gender roles, marriage, and fertility patterns which have unfolded over the past five decades. In the years following the Women's Movement of the 1960s, women and men have achieved parity in educational attainment, and women are increasingly likely to enter professional careers, and to demand more equitable division of household labor. These changes in gendered roles and opportunities inside and outside the home suggest that widowed men and women in future generations will face fewer challenges when grappling with household and practical tasks traditionally associated with the opposite gender.

Demographic and family changes also have critical implications for the context and consequences of spousal loss in future generations. Future cohorts of older adults are far more likely than current elders to have divorced and remarried. Compared to members of the CLOC sample, their late-life marriages may be slightly shorter-lived on average, but may also be marked by higher levels of closeness and warmth. Moreover, future cohorts of older adults will have significantly fewer children than members of the CLOC sample, given the declines and then stabilization in fertility rates that have occurred since the early 1960s. Ageing Baby Boomers will have fewer adult children than prior generations of elders; whether having fewer children leads to the receipt of less instrumental, expressive, or social support remains to be seen.

Limitations and New Directions

In this brief review, we have considered only a handful of the individual, dyadic, and societal-level factors that may affect how older adults experience spousal loss. Bereavement researchers face the challenge of identifying other conditions that protect against severe grief, anxiety, and social isolation, in order to best devise practical and culturally sensitive interventions. For instance, a growing body of research underscores the importance of religious, spiritual, and self-efficacy beliefs for coping with loss (Fry, 2001; Schaefer and Moos, 2001). By identifying the psychological resources that ease the widowhood process, practitioners can target interventions towards individuals who appear to lack such resources.

A further limitation of our review is that we have focused solely on the macrosocial context of the United States in the late twentieth and early twenty-first century. As such, our research findings and our speculations about future cohorts of bereaved elders apply primarily to persons in Western, individualistic nations similar to the United States. We would encourage researchers to consider how psychological reactions to loss may reflect a broader array of cultural contexts. For instance, the normative pressures to maintain an independent household and to be self-reliant and psychologically resilient following spousal loss may be particularly acute in cultures which emphasize individualism and autonomy, such as the United States. In collectivistic nations, such as Japan, the cultural emphasis on interdependence, and fulfilling the needs of others may enable a smoother widowhood transition (e.g., Markus and Kitayama, 1991). Other cultural factors, including patterns of household structure and filial piety (Ikels, 1993), and attitudes towards life and death may condition the experience of elderly bereaved. For instance, current Western notions of bereavement encourage breaking ties with the deceased, while other cultures, such as the Balinese, view sustained bonds to the deceased as an indication of the importance of the relationship and of one's own strength of character (Stroebe et al., 1992). As practitioners develop policies and interventions for the elderly bereaved, they must take into consideration the larger cultural, social, historical, and demographic backdrop against which spousal loss occurs.

Notes

1. The Changing Lives of OLder Couples (CLOC) study is supported by grants RO1AG15948 and P01-AG05561 from the National Institute of Aging.
2. The variation in the number of controls interviewed at the six- and 18-month follow-up interviews is due solely to the availability of funding.

References

Abramson, L. Y., Seligman, M., and Teasdale, J. (1978). Learned helplessness in humans: Critique and reformulation. *Journal of Abnormal Psychology,* 87, 49-79.

Anashensel, C. S., Pearlin, L. I., Mullan, J. T., Zarit, S., and Whitlach, C. (1995). *Profiles in caregiving: The unexpected career.* New York: Academic Press.

Antonucci, T. C. (1990). Social supports and social relationships. In R. H. Binstock and L. K. George (Eds.), *Handbook of aging and the social sciences* (3rd ed.). San Diego: Academic Press.

Archer, J. (1999). *The nature of grief: The evolution and psychology of reactions to loss.* London: Routledge.

Averill, J. R. (1968). Grief: Its nature and significance. *Psychological Bulletin,* 70, 721-748.

Beck, A. T. (1967). *Depression: Clinical, experimental, and theoretical aspects.* New York: Harper and Row.

Bianchi, S. (1995). The changing economic roles of women and men. In R. Farley (Ed.), *State of our union: America in the 1990s.* New York: Russell Sage.

Blauner, R. (1966). Death and social structure. *Psychiatry,* 25, 378-399.

Bonnano, G. A., Notarius, C. I., Gunzerath, L., Keltner, D., and Horowitz, M. J. (1998). Interpersonal ambivalence, perceived dyadic adjustment and conjugal loss. *Journal of Consulting and Clinical Psychology,* 66, 1012-1022.

Bowlby, J. (1980). *Loss: Sadness and depression* (Vol. 3). New York: Basic Books.

Bruce, M. L., Kim, K., Leaf, P. J., and Jacobs, S. (1990). Depressive episodes and dysphoria resulting from conjugal bereavement in a prospective community sample. *American Journal of Psychiatry,* 157, 608-611.

Byock, I. R. (1996). The nature of suffering and the nature of opportunity at the end of life. *Clinics in Geriatric Medicine,* 12(2), 237-252.

Carey, R. G. (1979-1980). Weathering widowhood: Problems and adjustment of the widowed during the first year. *Omega,* 10(2), 163-174.

Carr, D. (2003). A "good death" for whom? Quality of spouse's death and psychological distress among older widowed persons. *Journal of Health and Social Behavior,* 44, 217-234.

Carr, D., House, J. S., Kessler, R. C., Nesse, R., Sonnega, J., and Wortman, C. B. (2000). Marital quality and psychological adjustment to widowhood among older adults: A longitudinal analysis. *Journal of Gerontology: Social Sciences,* 55B(4), S197-S207.

Carr, D., House, J. S., Wortman, C. B., Nesse, R., and Kessler, R. C. (2001). Psychological adjustment to sudden and anticipated spousal death among the older widowed. *Journal of Gerontology: Social Sciences*, 56B(4), S237-S248.

Caserta, M. S., Lund, D. A., and Rice, J. A. (1999). Pathfinders: A self-care and health education program for older widows and widowers. *The Gerontologist*, 39, 615-620.

Cherlin, A. (1981). *Marriage, divorce and remarriage*. Cambridge, MA: Harvard University Press.

Costa, P. T., and McCrae, R. R. (1985). *The NEO personality inventory manual*. Odessa, FL: Psychological Assessment Resources.

Ferraro, K. F. (1984). Widowhood and social participation in later life: Isolation or compensation? *Research on Aging*, 6(4), 451-468.

Field, M. J., and Cassel, C. K. (1997). *Approaching death: Improving care at the end of life*. Washington, D.C.: Institute of Medicine.

Fooken, I. (1985). Old and female: Psycho social concomitants of the aging process in a group of older women. In J. Munniches and P. Mussen and E. Olbrich and P. G. Coleman (Eds.), *Life span and change in a gerontological perspective* (pp. 7-101). Orlando, FL: Academic Press.

Freud, S. (1917/1957). Mourning and melancholia. In J. Strachey (Ed.), *Standard edition of complete psychological works of Sigmund Freud, volume 14* (pp. 152-170). London: Hogarth Press and Institute of Psychoanalysis.

Fry, P.S. (2001). The unique contribution of key existential factors to the prediction of psychological well-being of older adults following spousal loss. *The Gerontologist*, 41, 69-81.

Futterman, A., Gallagher, D., Thompson, L. W., Lovett, S., and Gilewski, M. (1990). Retrospective assessment of marital adjustment and depression during the first two years of spousal bereavement. *Psychology and Aging*, 5, 277-223.

Gerber, I. (1974). Anticipatory bereavement. In B. Schoenberg and A. C. Carr and A. H. Kutscher and D. Peretz and I. K. Goldberg (Eds.), *Anticipatory grief* (pp. 26-31). New York: Columbia University Press.

Guralnik, J. M., Fried, L. P., and Salive, M. E. (1996). Disability as a public health outcome in the aging population. *Annual Review of Public Health*, 17, 25-46.

Ha, J. Carr D., Utz R. L. and Nesse, R. M. (in press). Older adults' perceptions of intergenerational support after widowhood: How do men and women differ? *Journal of Family Issues*.

Hill, C. D., Thompson, L. W., and Gallagher, D. (1988). The role of anticipatory bereavement in older women's adjustment to widowhood. *The Gerontologist*, 28(6), 792-796.

Hirschfield, R. M., Klerman, G. L., Lavori, P., Keller, M. B., Griffith, P., and Coryell, W. (1989). Premorbid personality assessments of first onset of major depression. *Archives of General Psychiatry*, 46, 345-350.

Holden, K. C., and Smock, P. J. (1991). The economic costs of marital dissolution: Why do women bear a disproportionate cost? *Annual Review of Sociology*, 17, 51-78.

Holmes, J. H., and Rahe, R. H. (1967). The social readjustment scale. *Journal of Psychosomatic Research*, 11, 213-228.

HUD. (1999). *Housing our elders: A report card on housing conditions and needs of older Americans*. Washington, DC.: United States Department of Housing and Urban Development.

Ikels, C. (1993). Chinese kinship and the states: Shaping of policy for the elderly. In G.L. Maddox, M.P. Lawton (Eds.). *Annual Review of Gerontology and Geriatrics: Focus on Kinship, Aging and Social Change*. New York: Springer.

Jacobs, S., Hansen, F., Berkman, L., Kasl, S., and Ostfeld, A. (1989). Depressions of bereavement. *Comprehensive Psychiatry*, 31, 218-224.

Jacobs, S., Kasl, S., and Ostfeld, A. (1986). The measurement of grief: Bereaved versus non-bereaved. *The Hospice Journal*, 2, 21-36.

Jacobs, S., Kosten, T., Kasl., S., Ostfeld, A., Berkman, L., and Charpentier, P. (1987-88). Attachment theory and multiple dimensions of grief. *Omega*, 88, 41-52.

Jacobs, S. C., Schaefer, C. A., Ostfeld, A. M., and Kasl, S. V. (1987). The first anniversary of bereavement. *Israel Journal of Psychiatry and Related Science: Special Issue: Grief and Bereavement*, 24(1-2), 77-85.

Kramer, D. (1996-97). How women relate to terminally ill husbands and their subsequent adjustment to bereavement. *Omega*, 34, 93-106.

Lopata, H. Z. (1973). *Widowhood in an American city*. Cambridge, MA: Schenkman.

Lund, D. A., Dimond, M. F., Caserta, M. S., Johnson, R. J., Poulton, J. L., and Connelly, J. R. (1985-86). Identifying elderly with coping difficulties after two years of bereavement. *Omega*, 16, 213-224.

Lund, D. E., Caserta, M. S., Dimond, M. F., and Shapper, S. K. (1989). Competencies, tasks of daily living and adjustments to spousal bereavement in later life. In D. A. Lund (Ed.), *Older bereaved spouses*. New York: Hemisphere.

Markus, H. and Kitayama, S. (1991). Culture and the self: Implications for cognition, emotion and motivation. *Psychological Review* 98, 224-53.

Mendes de Leon, C. F., Kasl, S. V., and Jacobs, S. (1994). A prospective study of widowhood and changes in symptoms of depression in a community sample of the elderly. *Psychological Medicine*, 24, 613-624.

National Center for Health Statistics. (1992). *Monthly vital statistics, report 41*. Washington, D.C.: U.S. Government Printing Office.

Neugarten, B., and Hagestad., G. O. (1976). Age and the life course. In G. Binstock and E. Shanas (Eds.), *Handbook of aging and the social sciences* (pp. 35-55). New York: Van Nostrand Reinhold.

O'Bryant, S. L. (1990-91). Forewarning of husband's death: Does it make a difference? *Omega*, 22(3), 227-239.

Parkes, C. M. (1985). Bereavement. *British Journal of Psychiatry*, 146, 11-17.

Parkes, C. M., and Brown, R. (1972). Health after bereavement: A controlled study of young Boston widows and widowers. *Psychosomatic Medicine*, 34, 449.

Parkes, C. M., and Weiss, R. S. (1983). *Recovery from bereavement*. New York: Basic Books.

Rando, T. A. (1986). A comprehensive analysis of anticipatory grief: Perspectives, processes, promises and problems. In T. A. Rando (Ed.), *Loss and anticipatory grief* (pp. 3-38). Lexington, MA: Lexington Books.

Roach, M. J., and Kitson, C. (1989). Impact of forewarning on adjustment to widowhood and divorce. In D. A. Lund (Ed.), *Older bereaved spouses: Research with practical applications* (pp. 185-200). New York: Hemisphere Publishing.

Rosenberg, H. M., Ventura, S. J., and Mauer, J. D. (1996). *Births and deaths, United States*, 1995. Monthly Vital Statistics, 45(3).

Rosenblatt, P. (1983). Bitter, bitter tears: Nineteenth century diarists and twentieth century grief theories. Minneapolis: University of Minnesota.

Sanders, C. M. (1982-83). Effects of sudden vs. chronic illness on bereavement outcome. *Omega* 13, 227-241.

Schaefer, J. A., and Moos, R. H. (2001). Bereavement experiences and personal growth. In M.S. Stroebe, R.O. Hansson, W. Stroebe, and H. Schut (Eds). *Handbook of bereavement research: Consequences, coping and care*. Washington, D.C.: American Psychological Association.

Siegel, K., and Weinstein, L. (1983). Anticipatory grief reconsidered. *Journal of Psychosocial Oncology*, 1, 61-73.

Singh, B., and Raphael, B. (1981). Postdisaster morbidity of the bereaved: A possible role for preventive psychiatry. *Journal of Nervous and Mental Disease,* 169, 203-212.

Sonnega, J. (2001a). Spousal personality and grief in the elderly widowed: who is missed? Paper presented at the Gerontological Society of America annual meeting, Chicago, IL.

Sonnega, J. (2001b). Special occasions and grief in the elderly widowed: Survey evidence confirms clinical wisdom. Ann Arbor: University of Michigan.

Stevens, N. (1995). Gender and adaptation to widowhood in later life. *Ageing and Society,* 15, 37-58.

Stroebe, M.S., Gergen, M., Gergen, K.J., and Stroebe,W. (1992). Broken hearts or broken bonds: love and death in historical perspective. *American Psychologist,* 47, 1205-1212.

Stroebe, M. S., Hansson, R. O., and Stroebe, W. (1993). Contemporary themes and controversies in bereavement research. In M. S. Stroebe and W. Stroebe and R. O. Hansson (Eds.), *Handbook of bereavement: Theory, research, and intervention* (pp. 457-476). Cambridge, England: Cambridge University Press.

Stroebe, M. S., Hansson, R. O., Stroebe, W., and Schut, H. (Eds.). (2001). *Handbook of bereavement research: Consequences, coping, and care.* Washington, DC: American Psychological Association.

Sweeting, H. N., and Gilhooly, M. (1990). Anticipatory grief: A review. S*ocial Science and Medicine,* 30, 1073-1080.

Teasdale, J. D., Taylor, R., and Fogarty, S. J. (1980). Effects of induced elation-depression on the accessibility of memories of happy and unhappy experiences. *Behavior Research and Therapy,* 18, 339-346.

Umberson, D., Wortman, C. B., and Kessler, R. C. (1992). Widowhood and depression: Explaining long-term gender differences in vulnerability. *Journal of Health and Social Behavior,* 33(1), 10-24.

United States Bureau of the Census. (1996). *Statistical abstract of the United States: 1996* (116th ed.). Washington, D.C: U.S. Government Printing Office.

University of Michigan Faculty and Staff Assistance Program. (2001). *Grief and loss: In the work place.* Ann Arbor, MI: University of Michigan.

Utz, R. L., Carr, D. S., Nesse, R. and Wortman, C. (2002). The effect of widowhood on older adults' social participation: An evaluation of activity, disengagement, and continuity theories. *The Gerontologist* 42(4), 522-533.

Utz, R., and Reidy, E., Carr, D., Kessler, R. C., Nesse, R. M. and Wortman, C. B. (in press). Changes in household following widowhood: A story of gender differences and dependence on adult children. *Journal of Family Issues.*

Volkart, E. H., and Michael, S. T. (1957). Bereavement and mental health. In A. H. Leighton and J. A. Clausen and N. A. Wilson (Eds.), *Explorations in social psychiatry.* London: Tavistock.

Waite, L., and Gallagher, M. (2000). *The case for marriage : Why married people are happier, healthier, and better off financially.* New York: Doubleday.

Warshawsky, M. (2000). Financing long-term care: Needs, attitudes, current insurance products, and policy innovations. *TIAA-CREF Research Dialogues,* 63.

Watson, M. A. (1994). Bereavement in the elderly. *AORN Journal,* 59(5), 1079-1084.

Webb, M. (1997). *The good death: The new American search to reshape the end of life.* New York: Bantam Books.

Wells, Y. D., and Kendig, H. L. (1997). Health and well-being of spouse caregivers and the widowed. *The Gerontologist,* 37(5), 666-674.

Wortman, C. B., and Silver, R. C. (1989). The myths of coping with loss. *Journal of Consulting and Clinical Psychology,* 57, 349-357.

Zisook, S., DeVaul, R., and Click, M. (1982). Measuring symptoms of grief and bereavement. *American Journal of Psychiatry,* 139, 1590-1593.

Zisook, S., Paulus, M., Shuchter, S. R., and Judd, L. L. (1997). The many faces of depression following spousal bereavement. *Journal of Affective Disorders*, 45(1-2), 85-94.

Zisook, S., and Shuchter, S. R. (1991). Early psychological reaction to the stress of widowhood. *Psychiatry*, 54, 320-333.

3

Re-Engaging: New Partnerships in Late-Life Widowhood

Nan Stevens

There are various myths and popular ideas but few empirical studies of gender differences in the tendency to form new heterosexual partnerships following widowhood in later life. Little is known about new partnerships actually developed by older widows and widowers. The few studies of remarriage in later life (see Bengtson et al., 1990) and one study of dating relationships of older single people (Bulcroft and Bulcroft, 1985) offer some information on new partnerships among the widowed.

The tendency of researchers to ignore remarriage and other kinds of new partnerships among middle-aged and older widowed people has been linked with ageism: "Socially and culturally their spouse's death may be seen as more acceptable and timely, and their remarriage as less socially meaningful," say Moss and Moss (1996: 168). Another reason that new partnerships have probably been of limited interest to researchers is that they are relatively infrequent and not always visible (Moss and Moss, 1996; Davidson, 1999). In Western countries like the United States and the Netherlands there are financial disincentives for older people to remarry since social security and old-age pensions are negatively affected by remarriage. When relationships between older couples are not registered as a marriage, they are difficult to trace and study. Thus very little is known about cohabiting or otherwise romantically involved older couples (Bulcroft and Bulcroft, 1985; Davidson, 1999).

Though research on new partnerships among widows and widowers is scarce, there are some widespread beliefs about this topic in relation to gender. Two beliefs are prevalent: (1) that older men "replace" their deceased partners more readily than older women and (2) that women "do better" on their own following widowhood and that therefore their desire for a new partner is less strong (Davidson, 1999). Examination of the available data on attitudes and actual practices in relationships reveals some evidence both to support and refute these ideas.

Demographic data from several Western countries show a regular pattern of gender differences in remarriage rates. In the United States about 20 percent of older widowers are remarried, compared to 2 percent of older widows (Bengtson et al., 1990). In Great Britain, the proportion of widowers who remarry after middle age is much higher than for widows in every birth cohort. At age fifty-five, the ratio of men to women who remarry is 5 to 1, and the ratio increases steadily with age (Davidson, 1999). One obvious explanation is the differential availability of potential partners for older widows and widowers. Since men have a lower life expectancy and women tend to marry men older than themselves, four to five times as many women as men are widowed in later life. However despite the larger pool of available women to choose from and despite the fact that more widowers than widows remarry, older widowers' rates of remarriage are low compared to younger cohorts of widowed men (Davidson, 1999).

A complex set of attitudes influences whether a widow or widower considers a new partnership as an option for the future. An important factor is the nature of the attachment to the deceased partner. It is now generally accepted that rather than relinquishing the tie to the deceased, the widowed maintain an inner representation of the deceased partner which is constructed and reconstructed during the process of adaptation to widowhood (Silverman and Klass, 1996). Some widowed people experience a continuing sense of the presence of the deceased; others have a tendency to idealize or "sanctify" the deceased partner (Lopata, 1996). In both cases, this kind of active tie to the deceased might interfere with the establishment of a new partnership. In one study widows were asked why they chose to remain single: the most common answer, reported by 40 percent, was that they had not found anyone as nice as their deceased husband (Gentry and Shulman, 1988). However the continued attachment to a deceased spouse is not necessarily a detriment to a new partnership. Moss and Moss (1996) have described how ties with deceased spouses are maintained in triadic relationships when widows and widowers remarry.

The importance of having and being a partner for an individual's sense of self influences his or her motivation to engage in a new partner relationship, as well as the importance attached to a lifestyle as a couple (Lopata, 1980). In a study of loneliness, Dykstra (1995) examined the importance of having a partner and the desirability of being single among formerly and never married older people. Widowers and divorced men rated being single as least desirable and gave the highest desirability rating to being partnered. Widows rated being single more positively than widowers and the desirability of being partnered less highly. These findings suggest that widowers are more motivated than widows to establish a new partnership and supports the popular belief that women "do better" by themselves in widowhood.

Another determinant of motivation for a new partnership is the widow's or widower's experience as a single person, especially the degree to which loneliness and deprivation are experienced due to the absence of the partner. Lopata (1980, 1996) has described loneliness as the most pervasive problem in the lives of the widowed. Widowed people often miss both the intimacy of the relationship with the partner and the social life that they led as a couple. Thus they are vulnerable to two forms of loneliness involving both emotional and social isolation (Weiss, 1973).

In a large representative survey of 4,000 people over age fifty-five, the loneliness of men and women in different groups according to marital status and marital history was compared (de Jong Gierveld and Dykstra, 1998). Those men and women still in their first marriage, widowers who had remarried, and women in Living Apart Together (LAT) relationships demonstrated the lowest loneliness scores (± 1.7); they were not lonely, since the cutoff point for loneliness is 3. Men and women who were cohabiting and male LATers were also not lonely, with scores between 2.4 and 2.7. Remarried widows were as lonely as widows who were living alone (3.1), and less lonely than widowers who were living alone (3.6). Widowed older women apparently do better in non-traditional partnerships, such as LAT relationships, while men seem to benefit more in new marriages. The authors point out that women are less likely than men to find emotional fulfillment in exclusive heterosexual relationships; they require additional close relationships, for example with children and friends, to fulfill their emotional needs. These may be easier to maintain in LAT relationships. When women remarry, they are more likely to suffer from conflicting loyalties.

> Presumably, women are more sensitive than men to the consequences of remarrying for relationships with friends, family members—and children in particular. Remarriage is likely to mean there is less undivided time, energy and attention for others than the partner, which may give rise to feelings of frustration and concern. (Dykstra and de Jong Gierveld, 2001: 4)

In a smaller qualitative study comparing widows and widowers, no significant difference was found between widows and widowers in the intensity of loneliness three to five years after the partner's death. This was true despite the fact that a higher percentage of widowers had developed new partner relationships, namely 38 percent of the men compared to 8 percent of the women (Stevens, 1995). Widows tended to intensify different kinds of relationships—with children, neighbors, and friends who were often widowed—to reduce their loneliness. The pool of available older women clearly offers men a greater chance of finding a new partner and women a greater opportunity for establishing new female friendships in widowhood.

One would expect that estimation of one's chances of finding a suitable partner will influence an individual's motivation to pursue this option. However, when widows were asked why they remained single, only 3 percent mentioned the lack of single men (Gentry and Shulman, 1988). In addition to the observation that they had not found anyone as nice as their husband, many said they liked being single and therefore would not remarry. In her study of ways in which older widows and widowers had reorganized their lives, Davidson (1999) found that many widows were not inclined to become involved with a new partner because they enjoyed their freedom and because they no longer wished to fulfill the traditional woman's role in marriage, that of servicing the needs of a man.

In this article several questions concerning new partnerships among widows and widowers in later life will be addressed: How many people choose to engage in new heterosexual partnerships following widowhood in later life? What kinds of heterosexual partnerships do older widows and widowers actually develop? Are new partnerships effective in fulfilling relational needs and reducing loneliness among older widows and widowers? How do widows and widowers with new partners integrate their continuing bond to their deceased partner in the new relationship?

Methods

Data from two studies are used to answer the research questions. The Dutch Aging Survey (DAS) was designed to gather information on the living conditions, well-being, and personal meaning systems of people in the second half of life. It involves a representative sample of 984 Dutch residents between the ages of forty and eighty-five who were living independently (Steverink et al., 2001). There were 130 widowed respondents (mean age 71.9), of whom 106 were widows and twenty-four widowers. One topic covered in the survey was social relationships. All single respondents were asked about the desirability of a new partner relationship. It is possible to examine associations between background variables, the desire for a new partner relationships, and loneliness. Unfortunately the survey does not offer information about actual new partner relationships.

The second study focused on ways in which older widows and widowers had reorganized their lives several years after the partner's death (Stevens, 1995). The sample of fifty widows and thirty-one widowers was drawn from the registry of a middle-sized city in the Netherlands (population 150,000). All respondents were between the ages of sixty and seventy-five; the mean age for widows was sixty-nine, for widowers sixty-eight. The respondents were living independently and had been widowed three to five years earlier.

Data was collected by means of a semi-structured interview that combined open questions, structured measures, and standardized instruments. Respondents identified their most important relationships and provided information on frequency of contact, shared activities, and exchange of social support within these relationships. A questionnaire on relational needs and desires was developed based on the relational functions of intimacy, social integration, reassurance of worth, nurture, reliable alliance, and guidance (Weiss, 1968). A Dutch loneliness scale that consists of five positive and six negative items assessing discrepancies in the area of desired relationships was included (de Jong Gierveld and van Tilburg, 1999). Scores range from 0 (not lonely) to 11 (extremely lonely); the cutoff score for loneliness is 3. This scale was also used in the DAS survey.

Secondary analysis of the data has been carried out for this article. Identification of new partnerships was possible by examining data on living situations, primary relationships, and relational needs and desires. The interviews of respondents who identified partners among their primary relationships, as well as those that had regular contact in cross-gender relationships, were examined more closely in order to determine the nature of the relationship. For heuristic purposes three types of partnerships were identified: consummate partners, steady companions, and service providers. These will be defined and described in more detail in the results.

Results

Desire for a New Partner

One way of determining whether widows and widowers are interested in a new partner relationship is to ask them directly, as was done in the Dutch Aging Survey. Among the widowed only 11 percent replied positively to the question on the desire for a new partner relationship, while 12 percent replied "not at the moment, maybe later." The majority, 75 percent, reported that they were not interested in a new partner. There were significant age differences: 22 percent of those under age seventy were interested in a new partner, compared to 7 percent of those over seventy. A slight gender difference was apparent, but was not significant: 16 percent of the widowers desired a new partner compared to 9 percent of the widows. Women did indeed appear to do better alone: 60 percent of the widows reported that they were satisfied with their single life, compared to 46 percent of the widowers. The widowed people who expressed a desire for a new partner were better educated and lonelier than those not desiring a partner, though both groups were lonely, with scores of 4.4 and 3.5 on the loneliness scale. Unfortunately, it was not possible to identify the number of widows and widowers who had successfully developed a new partner relationship within this sample.

Actual Partner Relationships: Consummate Partners

In the second study new cross-gender relationships that had been developed among widowers and widows were examined in order to study the prevalence and variations in new kinds of partnerships. The respondent's own definition of the relationship was important in distinguishing different types of partnerships. The first type of partnership to be identified was the consummate partnership. Respondents involved in this type of partnership referred to the other as his or her partner, husband or wife, or fiancé(e). There were variations in the amount of time couples spent together, whether or not they cohabited, and the legal status of the relationship. However those in consummate partnerships shared the following qualities: a long-term commitment to the relationship, public identification as a couple, openly acknowledged love for the partner, and involvement in regular sexual relations. The partner was a primary source of emotional intimacy.

Three widows and five widowers had developed new consummate partnerships; they represent 10 percent of the sample as a whole, or 6 percent of the widows and 16 percent of the widowers. Their age ranged from sixty-two to seventy, the average age being sixty-seven. The new partners involved were also widowed. One widow and one widower had married their new partners. One widow and one widower were cohabiting, the widow and her new partner planning to get married soon. One widow and three widowers were involved in LAT relationships.

The distinction between a LAT arrangement and living together was occasionally a fine one; one couple seemed to be together constantly, though they described themselves as living separately since they maintained separate homes. A second couple who saw one another at weekends were planning to marry within a few months, so their LAT relationship was a transitional arrangement. However, LAT relationships were also the result of a conscious decision by one or both partners not to live together. Marie, aged sixty-two, had been widowed three years when she ran into Tom, a widower whom she had known when they were both young adults. They had developed a close relationship during the last six months. She explained their separate living arrangements as follows:

> He's a lovely man, but I know him well and I couldn't have him living in my house. I couldn't stand being bossed around. He's extremely neat, can't stand to have anything on the table or on the floor. It would drive me crazy. I told him, "If I let you live here, we'd be fighting all the time." I'm very happy with him but I don't want him here all the time. Then I'd lose the freedom I have now.

Examination of data on relational standards revealed that all the new consummate partnerships are multifunctional. The partners were important as sources of security, reassurance of worth, love, and physical affection (including sexuality); they served as sounding boards and as companions for various activities. When couples lived together, the partner was someone who shared household tasks, as well as someone to take care of, thus fulfilling the need to nurture. Though the couples did not share parenthood, they were interested and involved with one another's children and grandchildren. Marie described the multifaceted nature of a consummate partnership, in response to the standard on security in relationships:

> Besides my children and my friends I now have Tom. We haven't been together long but I feel twice as secure already. You have someone to talk to, to consult. We go out together. That gives me security. Someone who is really close to you. Someone your own age. I don't want to bother my children. There are some things that they don't need to know...The last half year my life has changed. It's the same for him ... We're so attuned to each other. We both feel secure now. We take care of each other. You don't feel alone anymore. You have someone of your own. That is real security.

Other widows and widowers involved in consummate partnerships made similar statements on the importance of their new partner.

The continuing bond with the former spouse(s) was evident in most of these relationships, often symbolically (Moss and Moss, 1996). Couples regularly shared memories of their deceased spouses; their pictures were prominently displayed in their homes, with fresh flowers and candles nearby as a tribute to the deceased. Occasionally couples visited and jointly maintained the graves of their first spouses. The former marital relationship did not serve as a hindrance to the development of a new partner relationship; people managed to maintain the tie with the deceased partner and build a new relationship that gave their life purpose and helped them reduce loneliness. One seventy-year-old remarried woman reported:

> I no longer feel like a widow; Jack, my second husband, has changed that. I haven't forgotten my first husband. We were married for 35 years ... Nothing can take away my memories of him. I still miss him, I think about him every day. But at the same time I have a new bond. I'm no longer lonely.

A sixty-eight-year-old remarried widower met his new wife at a social club; it had only been six months since his first wife's death when they began seeing each other.

> I began this relationship because I feel that my children have a right to their own lives. I want to be independent of them as long as possible ... When I was alone, I realized that we're social beings, that we want to be involved with others ... Knowing that I mean a lot to my new wife, that I help take away her loneliness, has given my life meaning.

While enjoying his new wife's company, this widower has encouraged her to continue with activities that she was involved in before she met him, like going dancing on Sunday afternoons. He continues to be active in various organizations for retired people and in sports clubs that his wife does not belong to. He believes that each person should maintain his or her individuality in a new relationship.

> Each partner has a whole life behind them at this age; it's important to recognize that and take the past into account, to be able to talk about the past. When you marry for a second time, you do it for different reasons ... for 50% with your heart and 50% with your mind.

Rational planning as well as romantic feelings seem to be the basis of several consummate partnerships.

Another sixty-nine-year-old widower who was planning to get married in the next half year met his new partner, a fifty-six-year-old widow, during a large public event in the city where he lived. They shared an interest in walking long distances, playing bridge, visiting museums, and other cultural activities. There were a lot of emotional issues to resolve before they became engaged. Neither of them wanted to move out of their home and she lived in another city. They settled on buying two adjoining apartments that were being built in a town near where he lives. He remained emotionally attached to his first wife, whom he missed every day. He described the distinction between his first and second marriage as follows:

> It's not as if you can go back to your youth by getting married again. My first wife and I were 22 when we met; we were just beginning our lives as adults. We were strongly attracted to one another and planned to build a life together. Our four children gave us an incredibly strong bond. The new relationship is also important but not the same. For one thing you know it can never last long. If I live to be 80, then we have 10 years together. If I make it to 85, we'll have 15 years. But then you're really old ... it's a totally different relationship.

Occasionally new consummate partnerships were described as better than earlier marriages; in two cases the first marriages were not especially happy. A sixty-three-year-old widower described himself as in seventh heaven with his new partner whom he met at an evening for singles. For one thing, the sexual relationship was much better than in his marriage. They enjoyed social activities and vacations together, as well as long conversations. They complemented each other, supporting one another and providing security: "Neither of us feels like a widow or widower anymore. We both had a rotten period which we've put behind us. We're both so happy that life can be so beautiful."

In general loneliness was absent or quite low among those widows and widowers with new consummate partnerships (M 1.9, SD 2.4); some reported an occasional sense of emptiness due to missing the first partner. One widow, who had moved to Amsterdam to live with her new partner, missed her family and friends in her hometown and therefore scored rather high (7) on the loneliness scale.

Steady Companions

A second type of cross-gender relationship involves regular companionship in a variety of activities; frequency of contact varies between daily and several times a week. Participants in steady companion relationships had difficulty labeling their partner; the other is referred to as a "special friend," a "kind of a girlfriend," "the old man," or "a fine mate who happens to be a woman." Most of these relationships are long-term, having lasted for several years, and involve a clear commitment to maintain joint activities and involvement. Feelings of affection are expressed more often than love by the widowed involved in these relationships. Despite the fact that they spend a great deal of time together, steady companions draw a clear distinction between their current arrangement and their previous marriage or what is usually considered a partner relationship. Most of them are careful to explain that sexual relations are not part of the arrangement. One widower explained: "At our age sex doesn't matter; it's companionship that counts."

Seven respondents reported this type of relationship (8 percent). They ranged in age from sixty-three to seventy-three; their average age being sixty-eight. Six of the seven were widowers. The women chosen by the widowers as steady companions were divorcees and never-married women as well as widows; the widow had an older widower as her companion. Often the participants in this type of relationship were previously acquainted. In one case two neighbors became steady companions. The seventy-year-old widow saw her eighty-six-year-old neighbor, a widower, every day. Their spouses had died within six months of each other five years earlier, so they began to visit and comfort each other. It happened more or less automatically. They continued to have coffee together, talk, play cards, and occasionally go to the theater. She was well acquainted with his children, who liked to include her when they visited their father. Other neighbors gossiped about them, which upset her: "It's just pleasant, it's nice to spend time together. There's nothing dirty or bad about it."

Another sixty-nine-year-old widower had a woman friend who was his son's mother-in-law. She was divorced and had had a difficult life, so he liked to help her out. They had developed a pattern of seeing one another three times a week and talking on the phone every day. He took her grocery shopping and cooked a special dinner for her every Saturday. Afterwards they spent the evening watching television. Sometimes they took walks together or went to the theater. He helped her with jobs around the house. He had trouble describing the nature of their relationship: "It's not personal, it's not an affair, it's really a friendship. We assumed from the start that we wouldn't have an intimate relationship. It's more superficial, just pleasant."

Another widower, sixty-two, described a similar but more intense relationship. After his own wife's death from cancer, he had befriended the widow of a colleague. They spent a lot of time talking about their partners and crying together and these conversations helped him recover from his wife's death. Gradually he and Alice began to take part in various activities together like grocery shopping and sharing meals, visiting their respective children, and going walking or fishing. He reported: "That gives you a kick, being active. The fact that you mean something to her and vice versa. The presence of another person is often enough."

The two of them spent every day together, he had dinner at her house and always returned home at around 11 P.M. They also went on vacation together and were accepted everywhere as a unique kind of couple. His intention was not to become as attached to her as he was to his wife:

> I don't want to be attached to someone else, I have my reasons for that. I never want to have to go through what I went through with my wife. That was a once in a lifetime thing. I don't want to have the pain and sadness that I had with her, and I think I can prevent it. My children are closer to me than Alice. They're family. She's close, but in a different way.

Not every widower who had a steady companion was as satisfied as the previous widow and widowers. One seventy-two-year-old man had developed a close friendship with a sixty-three-year-old single woman while his wife was in a nursing home; he had hoped to marry this friend after his wife's death. However she had told him that she preferred to keep the friendship as it was. She liked her freedom and did not want to have to fix his meals or consult him every time she did something. He saw her almost every evening, visiting her for coffee. They often went out together and always had dinner together on Sundays. He took care of her garden and she took care of him when he was ill. She was very affectionate toward him, yet he complained: "I'm alone every night. That's not easy. I'm quite healthy and capable of living intimately with a woman. But I don't get a chance."

Apparently this had been going on for several years. Despite his frustration, he was not lonely thanks to his involvement with this woman friend.

Like the consummate partnerships, these relationships involving steady companionship served a variety of functions. They often provided a sounding board for discussion of daily matters and occasionally for more personal matters; they were a source of reassurance of worth and help with instrumental tasks.

As with the consummate partnerships, respondents emphasized the distinction between these relationships and the original partner relationship. Having a steady companion was as effective as a consummate partnership in protecting the participants against loneliness; the average loneliness was equally low (M 1.9, SD 2.8).

Service Providers

A third pattern involves a task-oriented relationship in which widows or widowers performed gender role-related services for a member of the opposite sex on a regular basis. It was less frequent; only three cases were found and they comprised one widow and two widowers. It is questionable whether such an exchange should be described as a partnership. The widow served two meals a day to an older widower who lived in the neighborhood; he had previously been her partner in card games. The man would stay for coffee and watch TV at her house between meals. She had hoped that he would accompany her on outings, but he refused to do so. She was very angry and disappointed about the arrangement; nevertheless she arranged her schedule around their meals. (This gendered distinction, between women wanting someone with whom to go out from the home, and men desiring someone to whom to come home is noted also by Davidson in this volume.) There were also two widowers who had more satisfactory contact with widowed neighbors who washed their clothes or did sewing for them, while they took care of odd jobs for the widow. Average loneliness in this subgroup was higher (M 4.7, SD 5.5) because of the extreme score of the widow. The two widowers were not lonely.

Failed Partnerships

Among the respondents there were also a couple of widowed people who had experienced the breakup of a consummate partnership. One man, seventy-five, had spent every weekend for two years with a new partner who was also widowed; they had taken vacations together, which he enjoyed very much. His tendency to compare her critically with his wife had led to her ending the relationship recently. He missed her and hoped that they would get back together eventually.

The widow who had moved to Amsterdam to be with her new partner called several months after the interview to report that she had ended the relationship and returned to her hometown. She missed her family and friends too much and the partnership had not developed as she had hoped. She asked the researcher to warn other widows not to move house for the sake of a man.

Discussion

Examination of cross-gender relationships of widows and widowers several years after the loss of the partner reveals considerable variation in the partnerships that develop in later life. For heuristic purposes three different types of "partnerships" have been identified based on the widowed person's own definition of the relationship and the relational functions served by the partner. These include (a) consummate partnerships in which the partner was the primary source of emotional intimacy, companionship, and instrumental help; a long-term commitment, public identification as a couple, regular sexual relations, and a variety of living arrangements were involved; (b) steady companions in which companionship was of primary importance, emotional intimacy varied, and sexual activity and cohabitation were absent; and (c) a pattern in which participants regularly exchanged instrumental services according to gender roles. This limited form of partnership was less frequent than the other two types. Altogether only 22 percent of the sample was involved in one of these forms of partnerships at the time the interviews were held.

The higher percentage of widowers who were involved in all three types of relationships is probably due to a combination of factors. In general, widowers tend to consider a partner relationship more desirable and singlehood as less desirable than do widows (Dykstra, 1995). Also, widowers are lonelier than widows when they remain on their own. This is probably due to the tendency of men to rely on their wives exclusively for emotional intimacy, while women tend to have other sources of intimacy and companionship beside their husbands (Arber and Ginn, 1993; Dykstra and de Jong Gierveld, 2001). In a study of younger widows and widowers, men were more eager to remarry (Lopata, 1980); presumably their motivation for other kinds of partnerships is also greater, continuing on into later life. The greater availability of women who remain single provides older widowers more opportunity to develop new cross-gender relationships while widows have more potential female friends.

For the men and few women who develop new partnerships, there is greater continuity in their lifestyles following widowhood; they resume aspects of their former lifestyle as a couple in varying degrees. The claim that men who become widowed simply replace their wives is a myth which cannot be justified. Widowers and widows draw a clear distinction between their earlier marriages and new partnerships, whether these are consummate partnerships, steady companions, or service-oriented relations. New partnerships are sought to relieve loneliness and to maintain independence rather than rely on one's children. Being important to another person gives life meaning, according to those involved in new partnerships. The decision to engage in a new partnership is seen as the best solution, the most rational way of dealing with one's life as a widowed person to those who make this choice. The deep love for and loyalty to the original partner remain intact for most of the widowed that were interviewed, even when they developed new consummate partnerships.

The finding that steady companion relations were as frequent among widowers as consummate partnerships was rather surprising. Perhaps limiting the relationship's intensity, avoiding sexuality and cohabitation, has to do with loyalty to the original partner. It may also be due to a decline in interest in sexuality (often among older women) or a decline in the ability to perform sexually due to effects of medication or illness among older men (Corby and Skolnick, 1980). It is noteworthy that age differences between those involved in the three types of partnerships are slight; age does not seem to determine which form of partnership develops in this sample with an age range of sixty to seventy-five.

Companionship was central in most of the partnerships that were identified. Sternberg (1988) has observed that companionate love, a combination of emotional intimacy and commitment rather than passion, is characteristic of long-term marriages; it also seems to characterize many of the new partnerships that these older widows and widowers developed, though there were occasional reports indicating the passionate nature of a new partnership.

There are various issues that have to be resolved if a new partnership is to develop and continue. These include

- agreeing on the form that the relationship will take
- whether sexuality will be involved
- whether or not to live together
- where to live together (if this is the choice)
- which activities the couple will share and which will be continued separately
- how to integrate the memories of and loyalty to the former partner in the new partnership without having them interfere with the relationship
- dealing with conflicting loyalties between children, friends, family (in law) on the one hand and the new partner on the other hand.

In addition to having to negotiate such issues with potential partners, many widows and widowers engage in a kind of internal dialogue involving different voices or selves: the self that is loyal to the original partner, the self that longs to be part of a couple, the sexual self, the independent self, the self as a parent (Hermans and Kempen, 1993). This kind of internal dialogue in which the advantages and disadvantages of involvement in a new partnership are weighed and considered was evident in the interviews, especially among the lonely widowed without a new partner.

The potential disadvantages included the chance of losing a partner again, having to care for an ill partner, the risk of being taken advantage of (sexually, financially, or as a provider of household services), and the likelihood that a new partner might compare unfavorably to the deceased husband or wife. One disadvantage was mentioned by widows who were not lonely, that is, losing the freedom that they had come to enjoy. Both in the survey and the more qualitative study the majority of widows and widowers claimed that they were not interested in a new partner relationship. From this perspective the various partnerships that have been described in this article can be viewed as uncommon achievements. A minority of widows and widowers have succeeded in developing satisfactory partnerships.

As this chapter is based on secondary analysis of existing data, the results may already be outdated. Consummate partnerships among the widowed may have become more common since this data was collected in the early 1990s. However, a more recent study of older widows and widowers during the first three years of bereavement found that they are still relatively rare: only 3 percent identified new partners among their social relations (van Baarsen et al., 2000-2001).

The older people in this study had found their new partners in ways similar to those used by younger cohorts: through contact advertisements, at events for singles, at public social events, or among existing acquaintances. As modern means of finding partners, such as through the Internet, become increasingly available to older people, the proportion actually developing new partner relationships in later life may increase. Variations in partnerships may increase as baby-boomers grow older and widowed people become more sexually active due to long-term effects of the sexual revolution and further development of medication in support of sexual activity in later life. Awareness of alternatives to a traditional marital relationship, such as LAT relationships, may tip the balance in the process of weighing the advantages and risks of engaging in new partnerships. Continuing research on the topic of new partnerships in widowhood is necessary to trace these developments.

References

Arber, S., and Ginn, I. (1993) *Gender and later life*. London: Sage.
Bengtson, V., Rosenthal, C., and Burton, L. (1985). Families and aging: Diversity and heterogeneity. In R. H. Binstock and L. K. George (Eds.), *Handbook of Aging and the Social Sciences* (pp. 263-287). San Diego, CA: Academic Press.
Bulcroft, K., and Bulcroft, R. (1985). Dating and courtship in late life: An exploratory study. In W. A. Peterson and J. Quadagno (Eds.), *Social bonds in later life* (pp. 115-126). Beverly Hills, CA: Sage Publications.
Corby, N., and Skolnick, R. (1980). Psychosocial and physiological influences on sexuality in the older Adult. In J. E. Birren and R. B. Sloane (Eds.), *Handbook of Mental Health and Aging* (pp. 893-921). Englewood Cliffs, NJ: Prentice Hall.
Davidson, K. (1999). *Gender, age and widowhood: How older widows and widowers differently realign their lives*. Ph.D. Thesis, University of Surrey, Guildford, UK.
de Jong Gierveld, J., and van Tilburg, T. (1999). *Manual of the loneliness scale*. Department of Social Research Methodology, Free University, Amsterdam.
de Jong Gierveld, J., and Dykstra, P. (1998). Eenzaam of niet eenzaam? Identificatie van eeenzaamheidsrisicogroepen onder oudere mannen in vrouwen [Lonely or not lonely? Identification of risk groups for loneliness among older men and women]. In M. I.

Broese van Groenou, D. J. H. Deeg, C. P. M. Knipscheer and G. J. Ligthard (Eds.), *VU Visies op Veroudering* (pp. 173-179). Amsterdam: Thecla Thesis.
Dykstra, P., and de Jong Gierveld, J. (2001). Gender differences in Dutch older adult loneliness. Paper for the 17th Congress of the International Association of Gerontology, Vancouver.
Dykstra, P. (1995). Loneliness among the never and formerly married: The importance of supportive friendships and a desire for independence. *Journals of Gerontology: Social Sciences*, 50B:5, S321-S329.
Gentry, M., and Shulman, A. D. (1988). Remarriage as a coping response for widowhood, *Psychology and Aging*, 3, 191-196.
Hermans, H. J. M., and Kempen, H. J. G. (1993). *The dialogical self: Meaning as movement.* San Diego, CA: Academic Press.
Lopata, H. Z. (1980). The widowed family member. In N. Datan and N. Lohmann (Eds.), *Transitions of Aging* (pp. 93-118). New York: Academic Press.
Lopata, H. Z. (1996). *Current widowhood: Myths and realities.* London: Sage.
Moss, M. S., and Moss, S. (1996). Remarriage of widowed persons: A triadic relationship. In D. Klass, P. R. Silverman and S. L. Nickman (Eds.), *Continuing bonds: New understandings of grief* (pp. 163-178). London: Taylor and Francis.
Silverman, P. R., and Klass, D. (1996). Introduction: What's the problem? In D. Klass, P. R. Silverman and S. L. Nickman (Eds.), *Continuing bonds: New understandings of grief* (pp. 3-27). London: Taylor and Francis.
Sternberg, R. J. (1988). Triangulating love. In R. J. Sternberg and M. J. Barnes (Eds.), *The psychology of love* (pp. 119-138). New Haven, CT: Yale University Press.
Stevens, N. (1995). Gender and adaptation to widowhood in later life. *Ageing and Society*, 15, 37-58.
Steverink, N., Westerhof, G., Bode, C., and Dittmann-Kohli, F. (2001). Dutch aging survey. *Onderzoekdesign and instrumenten.* [Research design and instruments.] Department of Psychogerontology, University of Nijmegen, Nijmegen, the Netherlands.
van Baarsen, B., van Duijn, M. A. J., Smit, J. H. Snijders, T. A. B., and Knipscheer, C. P. M. (2000-2001). Patterns of adjustment to partner loss in old age: The widowhood adaptation longitudinal study. *Omega* 44, 5-36.
Weiss, R. S. (1968). The fund of sociability. *Transaction,* 6, 36-43.
Weiss, R. S. (1973). *Loneliness: The experience of emotional and social isolation.* Cambridge, MA: MIT Press.

4

Gender Differences in New Partnership Choices and Constraints for Older Widows and Widowers

Kate Davidson

There has been substantial investigation of the psychology of bereavement in the early period following loss of a spouse (Glick et al., 1974; Kubler-Ross, 1975; Parkes and Weiss, 1983; Shuchter and Zisook, 1993), but relatively little work has been done on gender differences in the meanings of widowhood in the longer term (Stevens, 1995). This article arises from a small qualitative study of twenty-five widows and twenty-six widowers in the United Kingdom. The respondents were born before 1930 (at least sixty-five years old at time of interview in 1995/6), widowed for a minimum of two years, lived alone in the community, and had not remarried. These criteria were established because the original purpose of the study was to investigate how differently older men and women realigned their lives in the medium and long term after widowhood. The study does not therefore examine the motivations of those widowed persons who have remarried, but did interview people who were in Living Apart Together (LAT) relationships.

Little sociological research has been carried out on marriage relations of older people (Askham, 1994), and remarriage of older widows and widowers has suffered even greater neglect (Vinick, 1978; Greene, 1990). Remarriage for older people does not hold the same interest for the wider community or for social scientists or policy makers compared to the remarriage of younger people, especially those with young children. Studies of elderly widowed people indicate that widowers are more likely to remarry than widows (Greene, 1990). There are two principal reasons offered as to why the remarriage rate of widowers is so much greater than that of widows: one is demographic and the other is cultural. There are many more widows than there are widowers: in the United Kingdom, half of women over the age of sixty-five are widowed compared with only a sixth of men (Office of National Statistics, 1998). Even should a widow wish to establish a new relationship, her opportunities are reduced. This is compounded by the societal expectation, found in most cultures, that women will marry men older than themselves. This, it has been argued, excludes the majority of older widows who might wish to get married again (Burks et al., 1988). The largest gap in the literature about widows and widowers is of cross-gender, non-cohabitational relationships. These relationships in later life generally receive only a paragraph or two at most in studies of older people.

Method

The sample was not representative in terms of gender distribution. Men were deliberately over-represented since the purpose of the study was to make a direct comparison between the sexes. The sample was collected through a variety of sources, including health professionals, colleagues, friends, neighbors, and "snowballing." Five women but no men procured other respondents by this snowballing method. These five women identified ten widows and three widowers for interview. The willingness and ability of widows to talk to others about the interview and ask other widows to participate confirms Lopata's (1973) observation of a "society of widows" who meet and support each other, often on a regular basis. Each interview took place in the respondent's home and lasted between one and three hours. The interviews were tape-recorded and fully transcribed, after which they were analyzed with the aid of a qualitative software program.

The age range of both male and female respondents was between sixty-five and ninety-two. The average age for the women was seventy-five, compared to seventy-eight for the men: approximately two-thirds of the widowers were over the age of seventy-five years compared to half of the widows. The widowers had longer marriages on average; over twice as many widowers as widows reached their Golden Wedding Anniversary (fifty years). Conversely, the average length of widowhood for women was almost fourteen years and that for men was just over seven years. In this sample, the widows were more likely to be outright homeowners but the widowers had higher pension incomes and more savings. Also, the widows were twice as likely as the widowers to be in receipt of state benefits. The characteristics of the sample reveal that because women have a greater life expectancy, the men who outlive them tend to be older, have had longer marriages and a shorter period of widowhood.

Two widows had remarried; one had been a young war widow from World War II (1939-1945) and the other following divorce in her early thirties. Five of the widowers had been married for the second time after previous widowhood or divorce. Seven of the widowers, but no widows, had an LAT relationship at time of interview; one widower subsequently married his partner.

New Partnership Formation in Later Life

Hatch (1995) developed an analytical framework for explaining choices and constraints for cohabitation in a population of people over the age of forty-five years in the United States. This in turn was adapted from Dixon's (1971) theoretical framework for explaining age at marriage and proportions never marrying. Dixon originally identified three conditions which intervened between the social structure and marriage patterns. These were availability of mates, the feasibility of marriage, and the desirability of marriage. A description of the analytical framework for new partnership formation, developed from Hatch's model, is illustrated in figure 4.1.

The *availability* of partners is primarily a result of the sex ratio of people eligible for new partnership formation. *Feasibility* is determined largely by variables of age, health, and financial assets which influence selection of a partner. *Desirability* is the intensity of the motivation to form a new relationship, which in turn is frequently governed by societal and familial expectations. This is primarily determined by the alternatives to reformation of a "couple" and the extent to which the advantages outweigh the disadvantages of relinquishing an element of freedom and independence which comes with living solo.

This framework seems appropriate for examining new partnership formation in older widows and widowers. It can offer an extension and revision of the rather narrow explanations of demography and cultural expectations (social structure) by developing the issues of feasibility to include age, health status and financial resources,

Figure 4.1

Explanation for New Cross Gender Partnership Formation

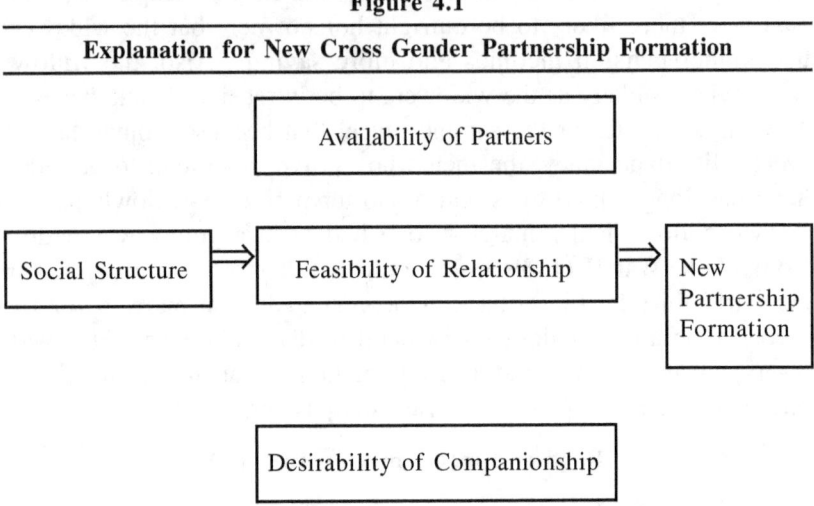

As developed by Hatch (1995:23) from Dixon (1971)

and desirability. It opens the discussion on choice and its relation to constraints in remarriage decisions.

Availability of Partners

Using data from marriage registrations in 2000 (Office of Population Censuses and Surveys, 2002a) and the mid-2000 population projections (Office of Population Censuses and Surveys, 2002b), remarriage rates were calculated in order to make a comparison between three age groups of older widows and widowers. Remarriage rates were calculated for divorced persons in the same age groups and examined for comparison.

Table 4.1 shows the remarriage rates of widowed (a) and divorced (b) people aged fifty-five and over in England and Wales in 2000. Widowed and divorced men were more likely than women to remarry in all the three age groups; however, the greatest differential is after the age of seventy-five.

The comparison between the remarriage rates of widowed and divorced women calls into question the principal theory offered to explain the low remarriage rates of older women, that is, the lack of available partners for older women. Divorced women between the

Table 4.1
Remarriage Rates (per 1000) by Age, England and Wales: 2000

(a) Older widowed men and women

Age Groups (yrs)	55 - 64	65 - 74	75+
Widowers	19.3	8.7	2
Widows	4.4	1.4	0.3
Ratio of remarriage rates of widowers to widows	**4:1**	**6:1**	**8:1**

(b) Older divorced men and women

Age Groups (yrs)	55 - 64	65 - 74	75+
Divorced men	33.3	14.3	6.2
Divorced women	12.5	3.3	0.5
Ratio of remarriage rates of divorced men to women	**2.6:1**	**4.3:1**	**12:1**

Author's Analysis
Sources: Marriage, Divorce and Adoption Statistics, FM2 No 28 (2002). Social Trends 32 (2002)

ages of fifty-five and sixty-four are three times as likely to remarry as widowed women (12.5 compared to 4.4). However, over the age of seventy-five, the likelihood of remarriage is only marginally greater (0.5 to 0.3). Interestingly, the ratio between remarriage rates of divorced men and women over the age of seventy-five increases dramatically to 12:1, compared to 8:1 for widowed men and women. Although there is still a very low probability of remarriage, divorced women between the ages of sixty-five and seventy-four are more likely to remarry than widowed men over the age of seventy-five (3.3 compared to 2). It would appear that for both women and men, but most particularly for widows, the choices and constraints regarding remarriage are as likely to be influenced by previous marital history as by the sex ratio of older people.

Feasibility of Relationship

Working from the literature on widowhood and remarriage, I have developed a model to demonstrate gender differences in the feasibility of remarriage, according to access to health, wealth and social network resources (figure 4.2). I argue that the model can be applied to other types of partnership formation for older widows and widowers, including cohabitation and LAT relationships.

Ill-health is not a significant barrier to the repartnering of widowers, so long as they are wealthy. Even if widowers are in poor health, as long as they command financial resources, the feasibility of new partnership formation is increased. However, if a widower has poor health and poor finances, the feasibility of new partnership formation is reduced. For widows, the presence of wealth is not as important as the enjoyment of good health in new partnership formation. Even if a widow has poor health and good financial resources, the feasibility of new partnership formation is reduced. A good social

Figure 4.2

Model Incorporating Gender into 'Access to Resources' in Relation to New Partnership Formation

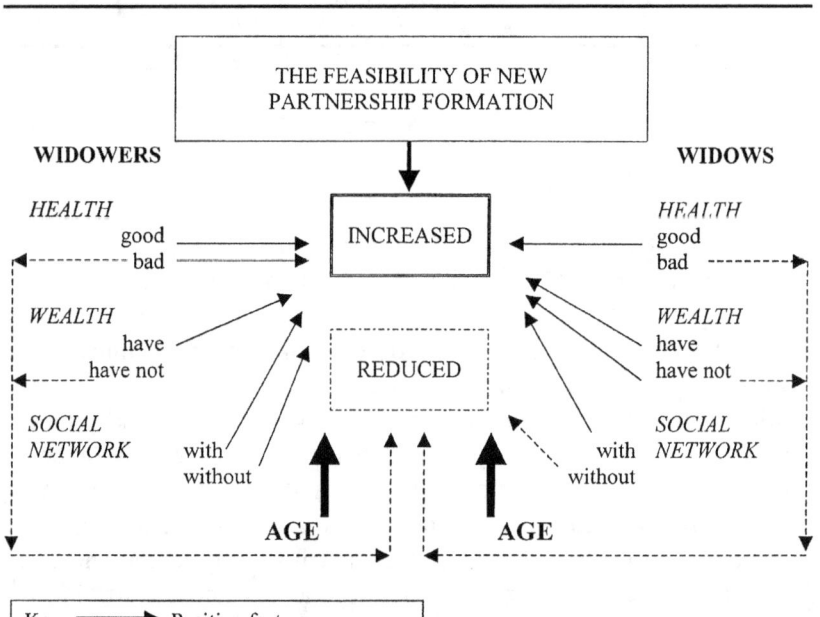

network is necessary for a widow to increase the likelihood of new partnership formation, but not as essential for a widower because he takes on the social network of his new partner (Greene, 1990). Advanced age in both sexes reduces the likelihood of new partnership formation, although as can be seen from the remarriage statistics, it happens at a much earlier age for women than for men.

Desirability of Companionship

Of the three intervening conditions, the desire for companionship is arguably the most influenced by social structure, which determines cultural and societal expectations and perceptions of appropriate age and gendered behavior. In most societies, there is an expectation that following bereavement, there is a period of mourning, although the timescale varies by culture (Lopata, 1996). This period, even within the same culture, is perceived to be shorter for men than for women: it is more acceptable for a widowed man than a woman to seek another companion at an earlier stage after bereavement (Campbell and Silverman, 1987). Thus has arisen "our prevailing wisdom ... that women grieve and men replace" (ibid: 3). Arber and Ginn (1993) suggest that cross-gender friendships are rare for older women, especially widows, but there is evidence to suggest that widowers have friendships with younger and older women who are single, divorced as well as widowed (van den Hoonaard, 2001; Moore and Stratton, 2002).

For the present older cohort of widows and widowers (those born during the first three decades of the twentieth century and socialized with Victorian, Judeo-Christian values), marriage is perceived as the only acceptable province within which to conduct an intimate relationship.

However, as shown earlier, relatively few widowed people remarry in late life. To date there has been little research exploring the wish for, the importance attached to, and gender differences in, the experience of romantic liaisons of older widows and widowers who maintain separate homes but visit each other, including overnight; socialize together; carry out daily routine activities together such as shopping, cooking, and eating; as well as going on holidays together. In younger couples, this relationship is usually one of the stages towards singling out a partner which usually leads to co-residence, whether marriage or cohabitation (Morgan, 1996). The following section explores data from my study comparing gender differences in the experience of late-life widowhood, including the desire to embark on a new relationship.

Findings

The principal theme to emerge from the study was of new partnership formation and the constraints and choices around sharing one's life again. With one exception, a widow, all the men and women spoke of loneliness as one of the hardest things to bear after the death of a spouse, even if the marriage or the final years had not been particularly happy. An antidote to this state would seem to involve finding another partner to share one's life. Many of the respondents said they would like a cross-gender companion, but on their terms. These terms were noticeably age and gender specific.

When asked if they had considered getting married again, the widows were more likely than the widowers, much as we would expect from the trend in the demographic data, to say that they had not considered remarriage (table 4.2).

Table 4.2 is divided into three broad answers: "Yes," "Perhaps," and "No." "Perhaps" was sub-divided for replies that involved widows and widowers who had also at some time considered remarriage but no longer. This was done to accommodate the diversity in the gendered meanings of "perhaps." The women were primarily retrospective in their answer ("I might have once") whereas the men tended to be more prospective ("if the opportunity arises").

Only one widow and two widowers were positive that they would like to get married again. Wealthy and childless, the widow and her husband had enjoyed a full social life before the bouts of severe depression he suffered for ten years and the diagnosis of Alzheimer's

Table 4.2

"Have you considered getting married again?"

		Widows n=25	Widowers n=26
1	Yes	1	2
2a	Perhaps in the past (if I had found the right person)	4	4
2b	Perhaps now (if I find the right person)	0	7
3	No	20	13

Disease three years before his death. She continued to socialize in mixed-sex groups, the Bowls Club and a Bridge Club, as well as have good contact with female friends, but she felt that in remarriage she would regain the status which permits, or is central to, the inclusion in a couple-orientated social life. Ingrid (pseudonyms are used throughout) wanted someone with whom she could go out, and considered her aloneness rather than her loneliness to be the problem:

> *Ingrid:* I think I would quite like to, if I found the right person. For the companionship really. It's awful—you never get invited as a single woman anywhere. Or if you do you think, "Oh Lord, I'm a bit de trop, on my own." But if Mr. Right came along I might consider it. *(Mrs. IG, seventy-four)*

For the widowers on the other hand, it was the loneliness they found unbearable:

> *Richard:* Yes, I'd be delighted to. I mean, the trouble about being on your own is, it doesn't matter how busy you are, at times, you are very lonely. And certainly if the right person came along, I would be only too pleased to get married. Just like that. *(Mr. RH, seventy-six)*

Joe (sixty-five) had been widowed twice, both his former wives having died of cancer. He had a relationship with a widow aged sixty-two, with whom he had struck up a friendship at church within weeks of being widowed for the second time, just over two years previously. Although well able to look after himself, which he had done while both his former wives had been ill and subsequent to their deaths, he said he hated living alone and actively looked for someone with whom to share his life. Joe had gone to a dating agency after the death of his first wife and through them had met his second wife:

> *Joe:* 'Cos I didn't like being on my own. This being on my own, I found it very difficult. You can easily slide into the drinking, which I did. ... I was going stir crazy of an evening, so I thought, "I've got to meet someone and start getting out again." And that's why I did that *(contact a dating agency)*. ... I can live on my own, I can do everything, I can cook and everything. But I like company. I think loneliness—to be on your own. I thought, there's other people out there like me, so why not two people to be happy? *(Mr. JE, sixty-five)*

Even though these three people expressed a strong desire to remarry, there were gender differences in that Ingrid wanted someone with whom to go out, whereas Richard and Joe wanted somebody to whom to come home.

Equal numbers (four) of the widowers and widows said they would have considered getting married again when they were younger, if they had found the right person. Geoffrey (seventy-five), Tom (seventy-six), Malcolm (seventy-five), and Henry (seventy-four), considered they were now "too set in my ways" or "nobody would want me now." These men had been widowed between six and fifteen years and all had been widowed before they were seventy. As their length of widowhood extended they became accustomed to solo living, and they became less inclined to want to remarry.

Of the four widows who no longer entertained the possibility of forming a new exclusive relationship, Cynthia (sixty-six) had gone to a dating agency and Rosie (seventy-eight) had gone to "singles" parties. Both spoke of disappointment. Cynthia's husband suffered from Alzheimer's Disease eight years before his death five years previously. Ten years before her husband's diagnosis, her eldest son was involved in a hang-gliding accident and was now tetraplegic. She nursed him when he came out of rehabilitation until her husband required constant care. She felt she had "missed out a lot of fun" during the almost twenty years she had cared for the two men. She had met several men through the dating agency and was looking for some romance, to go out to meals, to receive flowers, and have some male friendship:

> *Cynthia:* I met these men, they either had arthritis of the ankle, or they wanted to go to bed with you, and anything like that doesn't interest me any more. My husband went impotent when I was 42. So I'm not interested in sex. ... They'd drink your coffee and they'd have a nightcap. They they'd come out and eat your food, have a couple of whiskies after—that's all they wanted. Never wanted to take you out for a meal. Never wanted to bring you a bunch of flowers. ... *(They)* did nothing but talk about their dead wives. What an experience, I could write a book about it! *(Mrs. CF, sixty-six)*

She had no particular wish to remarry when she joined the agency, but wanted some fun in her life again, and if she found someone, she said she would consider remarriage. She stopped seeing these men as she felt they were "using" her not only to get a decent home-cooked meal, but also to provide a shoulder to cry on. Once again, the above quotation highlights the different gender expectations from a relationship: for women it was the wish for companionship *outside*, and for men, *inside* the home.

Rosie, widowed at fifty, was persuaded by friends to go to some "singles" meetings:

> *Rosie:* Holy smoke—that put me off men forever! The most revolting lot of things you have ever seen in your life. I mean, what do they want? One thing! "Let me take you back to have coffee." Not my scene at all. I love a laugh and a joke. I'll have a drink with anybody and that's that. *(Mrs. RD, seventy-eight)*

Winnie (seventy-eight), was widowed at the age of thirty-six and left with two daughters under the age of eight. She would very much have liked to get married again but she either liked (or was pursued by) men who were already married, or men who did not want to take on the responsibility of children:

> *Winnie:* They wanted to marry me. But I used to say "Well, I've got two little girls." And they would never mention the girls, never even ask to see them. ... And if you can't get on with the children, or won't accept them, it's out...(*With the married men*), either I didn't want to be the "other woman" or I didn't want to bring the children into that kind of situation. The children were my first priority. And that's really why I never married again. *(Mrs. WF, seventy-eight)*

Cynthia and Rosie were not alone in believing that the men they met were pursuing them out of self-interest, which included sex as well as being a housekeeper.

> *Sarah:* I could have. I had three proposals of marriage. But one I found out—and I'm glad I didn't. ... One of them was a gambler, which I never knew. Kept it very quiet from me until just accidental, somebody said to me, "Did you know... ?" And then the other one was ... Oh Lord! When he was with me he was all over me and that kind of thing but he was just for himself, self, self, self. Wanted somebody to marry to look after and to wash his clothes, iron, cook and look after him while he went out. *(Mrs. SD, seventy)*

All four of these women were widowed comparatively young, Winnie at thirty-eight, Sarah at forty-eight, Rosie at fifty, and Cynthia at sixty-one. None had found a man to whom they felt they could get married and none expressed any regret at not having done so. Sarah's daughter did not approve of her mother's wish for a new relationship—she threatened to refuse to let her see her grandchild again—and this was also a deterrent for her. The forty-eight respondents who did not *positively* desire remarriage were asked what were the reason for not having remarried. Their replies are shown in table 4.3.

From table 4.3 it can be seen that the widows were far more prepared than the widowers to engage in a discussion about their reasons for not having remarried, volunteering seventy-eight responses to the widowers' twenty-eight. The widowers tended to give one reason, and then close out the question. Most of the widows gave several reasons and the most frequently offered was that they did not want to look after another man (90 percent), followed by the contention that nobody could take their dead husband's place (80 percent). The latter finding supports the work of Moss and Moss (1980), who report on the strength of the tie of the deceased spouse in decision making about repartnering. Most of them said they had

Table 4.3

Frequency of Reasons Given for not Having Remarried by Gender

Reason given	Widows n=25	Widowers n=26
Does not want to look after another	22	0
Cannot replace spouse	20	9
Enjoyment of freedom	14	0
Not want to repeat unhappy marriage	5	0
Never fancied anyone (widows) Not met the right person (yet) (widowers)	3	8
Discouraged by adult children	4	0
Too set in ways	3	3
Not want sex	5	0
Nobody would want me now	2	7
Problems of inheritance	0	1
Total number of responses	78	28
Average number of responses	3:1	1:1

been happy to care for the spouse they married when young, with whom they had grown old. It was not just the prospect of nursing a sick partner to which they objected, but also the day-to-day work entailed in cooking, cleaning and washing which they were unprepared to take on. Mary (seventy) sums up the response of many of the widows to the prospect of remarriage:

> *Mary:* I just couldn't be bothered, I mean. It would have to be an old man for a start, I mean I'm seventy. Who wants to marry a man about seventy-five? Oh, I couldn't go to bed with an old man like that. I couldn't bear the thought of it. No. No thanks. Yes, and why should I lumber myself with another man? I'll have to cook for him, wash for him, go to bed with him. Oh no I couldn't be bothered with that. *(Mrs. MB, seventy)*

Most of the widows could not imagine taking on the responsibility of "an old man." In this was the assumption that the person who they would marry would be older than themselves, thus reflecting the culturally accepted norm of a man marrying a younger woman.

Even some who had been widowed when they were older said that they had "had their chances." Odette (seventy-nine), Joy (ninety-two), and Alice (eighty) spoke of widowers with whom they were friendly, and whom, had they chosen to pursue the matter, they could have married even though the widowers had said nothing openly:

> *Odette:* He never actually asked me but I am sure I could have married him if I had wanted to. But I didn't want to. *(Mrs. OD, aged seventy-nine)*

> *Joy:* From the Dancing Club, yes. I could have had him, if I'd wanted. But I didn't want to. *(Mrs. JW, ninety-two)*

They spoke of female friends and acquaintances who had remarried and who had experienced unhappiness as a result.

> *Joy:* Well, it's up to them if they want to take a chance. Some people I know have married again and they've regretted it. *(Mrs. JW, ninety-two)*

Some related, at length, "cautionary tales" of these unsuccessful remarriages of widows in justifying their decision to remain alone, despite the pressures from men they knew and perceived normalcy of a couple-orientated society. The "cautionary tales" were not so much about marital or familial conflict, but frequently about the fact that these women ended up looking after sick men.

Widows also did not want to repeat the process of acquiring what Howard and Hollander (1997) refer to as a "homemaker's investments": learning over a period of time the likes and dislikes of a new husband, or promoting and maintaining bonds with his family. These "investments," they point out, are not easily transferable to another relationship. The "capital" brought into a marriage by a man, namely, financial resources, prestige and social status, is more easily transferred to another relationship. When men remarry, they feel they can offer financial security, protection, and security at home. For example, Richard, wealthy and childless, wanted to remarry. He said he would like to leave his money "somewhere nearer home" than nieces, nephews, and godchildren.

The difference between what is brought to a relationship ("marriage capital" of men) and what is subsequently put into a relationship ("homemaker's investment" of women) proved to be fundamental to gender difference in remarriage choices and constraints for the widowed men and women in this study. The women did not want the "bother" of acquiring this new information and associated work, and were adamant that they were enjoying a freedom they had no wish to relinquish. They also saw themselves as having become "selfish" and this selfishness was frequently allied to feelings of guilt.

> *Sally:* Yes, there is freedom to do what I want—but it's being awfully selfish! *(Mrs. SH, seventy-one)*

> *Celia:* Don't worry, I am content leading my own life. I think it's pure selfishness actually, not wanting to look after somebody again. *(Mrs. CT, seventy-five)*

Generally speaking, the widows thought selfishness was a bad thing and expressed some guilt about it.

> *Cynthia:* I don't want to take the responsibility of washing for somebody and ironing for somebody. And I can do what I want to do. It is selfish, absolute selfishness. ... I feel a bit guilty sometimes. *(Mrs. CF, sixty-six)*

To summarize, many of the widows felt that not having to consider anybody else, certainly not as intensely as they would a spouse, was a benefit of being widowed and a compelling reason for not wishing to establish a new partnership (Davidson, 2001).

New Partnerships After Widowhood

The widows had no desire to get married again because they had no wish to look after another man and also because they considered that their dead husband could not be replaced. The word "replaced" here is at the crux of the difference between how men and women viewed a new cross-gender relationship. Although both genders used the words "cannot replace," analysis revealed that it had different meanings for men and women. For many of the widows, it meant that there could be no other person at all, in any capacity: there could be nobody instead of their husband. For the widowers, it meant that they would not find another person like their dead wife, but there may be somebody they could care about and love *in addition to* but *not instead of*, their late wife. In other words, for the widowers, the person was irreplaceable, but not the role they carried out as wife, friend and companion.

Seven of the widowers but none of the widows had a cross-gendered relationship at the time of interview and all but Michael (ninety-one) were under the age of seventy-five. In the sample of widowers, there were eight aged seventy-four or under, and six of these currently had a cross-gender relationship. All six of these widowers were home owner-occupiers and had occupational pensions.

Five of them considered themselves to be "very comfortable" financially and enjoying good health. None of these six men wished to get married again at the time of interview. Eric (seventy-four) and Paul (seventy-three) would not rule out the possibility, but at present it was not what either they or their partners wanted. Les (sixty-eight) said his partner would very much like to get married, but it was he who was unwilling:

> Int: Do you think she would like to get married?

> *Les:* She wants to, yes. I don't want to. It's very difficult. I don't want to hurt her, but the whole time I have to sort of hold her back, you know. ... Friendship, fine, but that's it. She wants marriage, but there's no way. *(Mr. LE, sixty-eight)*

Henry (seventy-four) said his partner had discussed marriage, but he was no longer interested in remarrying because he had grown accustomed to living alone and "doing his own thing." The primary reason given is because marriage "didn't feel right" although they were happy to have a friendship and in Ian's (seventy-two) case, a sexual relationship which did not involve marriage.

> *Ian:* I can accept a relationship, sure. Marriage, no, I can't imagine it. I can't. Because I'd compare all the time. And I'd feel guilty. ... I'd feel guilty that I wasn't in love with the person that I married. *(Mr. IC, seventy-two)*

It would seem then that these widowers were more prepared than the widows to embark or "take a chance" on a new relationship. Although none was cohabitational (as per the remit of the research design), the relationships they described included some degree of physical intimacy and the younger the widower, the more likely it was to involve sexual intercourse.

Roberts and Sinclair (1978) described a similar arrangement for younger Jamaican couples, as a "visiting union." The features in this relationship are identified as the existence of a steady sexual relationship, the maintenance of separate households, and the lack of legal sanction of the union. There are some parallels with the LAT relationships of older people, with the exceptions of the importance of sexual intercourse, the presence of young children and, in Roberts and Sinclair's study, the union more frequently led to marriage. Levin and Trost (1999) and Ariza and De Oliveira (1998) identify an increase in LAT relationships in Northern Europe. These non-co-residential arrangements are frequently made by divorced couples, but also by people who are widowed, who desire a relationship but wish to retain independence and autonomy. More recently, Borell and Karlsson (2000) and in this volume identify LAT as a developing choice of relationship arrangement for older people in Sweden.

In Jamaica, the preference for meeting in the home of the woman rested with the likelihood of her having children and was seen as more convenient (Roberts and Sinclair, 1978). For the older men in my study, the preference was also the woman's home because she offered the more "homely" surroundings and she was familiar with her kitchen when she produced meals. The outside entertainment also often revolved around going out for a meal. Men saw this as a way of reciprocating meals they received from their partners, particularly if the men were not keen to cook themselves.

Beryl lived in sheltered accommodation and was the only widow in this study to have had a relationship following bereavement. It had lasted ten years but had recently ceased owing to his ill-health:

Beryl: Well, so see up 'til a little while ago, a few weeks, I had this gentleman friend. It was a very nice way of living. We shared our lives. He lived not far from here and he got a very nice little house, little garden. Very nice and he's a very, very nice gentleman to be with. *(Mrs. BL, eighty-three)*

The "gentleman friend," Gilbert, had been a neighbor for several years and his wife had died about six months before Beryl's husband. They gave each other support and help during that year and they had started an exclusive friendship. She described the pattern of their lives:

Beryl: He would come here. I would cook the meal but then we'd go back to his house in the evening. I would go and sleep in his house, he had three bedrooms, plenty of room. And we'd rise in the morning, then we'd have breakfast in his house. ... If we weren't going anywhere special, like, he'd run me home to do whatever I liked, see my friends or what. ... It was a very nice way of living. See, I had the freedom of the car and a nice—and we had lots of holidays together, him and I. We went to New Zealand to see my brother.

Int: Did you ever think of getting married?

Beryl: Gilbert's family said, "Why don't you ... ?" No, I didn't want to ... I don't know why. There was only one person I married and I was happy about that. I don't know why, 'cos it might have worked out good. But then again it couldn't have done because Gilbert wasn't able to look after himself and I was a bit worried. I thought, well, I can't look after ... well, as you get older, can you? Your husband, that you've had for years, you don't think about nursing do you? But that's it...When I go to sleep at night, it's Jack *(husband)* I think about. Not Gilbert, we didn't have that sort of—you know. *(Mrs. BL, eighty-three)*

Almost all (96 percent) the widows compared to half (54 percent) the widowers said that at the time of interview, they had no intention of forming a cross-gender relationship. Interestingly, twelve of the widows said they would like to have a male friend, especially if he had a car, for shopping and outings. When I asked them why they did not pursue such a friendship, they said that they did not want to put themselves in a position where they might eventually be required to "look after" a man. They did not want any more cross-gender "obligations." This might entail doing his ironing and cleaning his house, and having intimate sexual relations. Overwhelmingly, they saw "strings attached" to any relationship and were not prepared to compromise their current freedom.

> *Alice:* A widower moved into the flat upstairs a few months ago and he has been very friendly indeed. I thought to myself, "He's not getting his feet under my table and that's definite." You know what I mean. I had a husband and five children and that's enough in any woman's lifetime. *(Mrs. AS, eighty)*

The most important factors in determining the wish to form a new partnership were gender and age: these older widows, regardless of present age, age at spouse loss or length of widowhood, did not generally wish to form an exclusive relationship. For the widowers, the decision was largely predicated on their age and health status: the older and frailer the widower, the less feasible the prospect of a new cross-gender relationship. Also, the longer he had been married before bereavement, and consequently the greater the age at loss, the less he wished for another woman in his life.

Conclusion

Dixon's (1971) original analytical framework, developed by Hatch (1995), was used in this study to examine the choices and constraints of repartnering for older widows and widowers. This model identifies three intervening conditions to explain age at marriage and proportions never marrying: availability of mates, feasibility, and desirability. My research has shown that these intervening conditions are gendered when applied to relationship choices of older widowed people. Availability of mates affects women: there are far fewer partners available for older widows than older widowers, given cultural norms about gender differences in the age of partners. Older widowers are much more likely than widows to desire a new relationship; therefore, feasibility is more likely to affect widowers who would like to establish a new relationship: the older, frailer and poorer the widower, the less likely he is to attract a partner.

As noted earlier, widows and widowers who were currently remarried or cohabiting were not interviewed, although five of the widowers and two widows had been married more than once. Thus, it is not possible, nor is any claim made, for generalization to the wider widowed population. However, age- and gender-specific differences in attitudes to and desire for new partnership formation emerged from the analysis.

Virtually all the widows in this study did not wish for a new relationship, regardless of age, health or wealth status. The men were more likely to wish for, or had embarked upon a romantic cross-gender relationship—and the younger, healthier, and wealthier the widower, the greater the likelihood of this.

The principal reasons advanced by the widows for not wanting a new relationship were that they did not wish to look after another man, that they had had a happy marriage, and that their late spouse could not be replaced. In order to care for and care about another man, they would have to relinquish the freedom and independence they had enjoyed since coming to terms with living alone. This leads me to conclude that contrary to the commonly held view that older widows do not have new partnerships primarily because of the lack of available mates (Burch, 1990; Blom, 1991; Askham, 1994; Hatch, 1995), an important intervening condition is *choice*: the older widows in this study did not desire a new relationship.

References

Arber, S., and Ginn, J. (1993). *Gender and later life: A sociological analysis of resources and constraints.* London: Sage.

Ariza, M., and De Oliveira, O. (1998). *Contrasting scenarios: Family formation and woman condition in the Caribbean and West Europe.* Paper presented at the International Sociological Association World Congress, Montreal, Canada.

Askham, J. (1994). Marriage relationships of older people. *Reviews in Clinical Gerontology,* 4, 261-268.

Blom, I. (1991). The history of widowhood: A bibliographic overview. *Journal of Family History,* 16(2), 191-210.

Borell, K., and Ghazanfereeon Karlsson, S. (2000). *Living Apart Together in old age. Women's boundary making and the social construction of home.* Paper presented at the British Society of Gerontology annual meeting, Oxford, UK.

Burch, T. (1990). Remarriage of older Canadians. *Research on Aging,* 12(4), 546-559.

Burks, V. K., Lund, D. A., and Dimmond, M. (1988). Bereavement and remarriage in older adults. *Death Studies,* 12, 51-60.

Campbell, S., and Silverman, P. (1987). *Widower: When men are left alone.* New York: Prentice Hall.

Davidson, K. (2001). Late life widowhood, selfishness and new partnership choices: A gendered perspective. *Ageing and Society*, 21(3), 279-317.

Dixon, R. (1971). Explaining cross-cultural variations in age at marriage and proportions never marrying. *Population Studies,* 25(July), 215-233.

Glick, I., Weiss, S., and Parkes, C. M. (1974). *The first year of bereavement.* New York: John Wiley and Sons.

Greene, R. W. (1990). *The positive effect of remarriage on older widowers' well-being: an integration of selectivity and social network explanation,* University of Michigan: Ann Arbor MI.

Hatch, R. G. (1995). *Aging and cohabitation.* New York: Garland.

Howard, J., and Hollander, J. (1997). *Gendered situations, gendered selves.* Thousand Oaks, CA: Sage.

Kubler-Ross, E. (1975). *On death and dying.* New York: Macmillan.

Levin, I., and Trost, J. (1999). Living apart together. *Community, Work and Family,* 2, 279-294.

Lopata, H. Z. (1973). *Widowhood in an American city.* Cambridge, MA: Schenkman.

Lopata, H. Z. (1996). *Current widowhood: Myths and realities.* Thousand Oaks, CA: Sage.

Moore, A., and Stratton, D. (2002). *Resilient widowers.* New York: Springer.

Morgan, D. (1996). *Family connections.* Cambridge, UK: Polity.

Moss, M., and Moss, S. (1980). The image of the deceased spouse in remarriage of elderly widow(er)s. *Journal of Gerontological Social Work*, 3(2), 59-70.

Office of National Statistics (1998). *Annual Abstract of Statistics.* London: HMSO.

Office of Population Censuses and Surveys (2002a). *Marriage, Divorce and Adoption Statistics.* London: HMSO.

Office of Population Censuses and Surveys (2002b). *Social Trends* 32. London: HMSO.

Parkes, C. M., and Weiss, R. (1983). *Recovery from bereavement.* New York: Basic Books.

Roberts, G., and Sinclair, S. (1978). *Women in Jamaica: Patterns of reproduction and family.* New York: KTO Press.

Shuchter, S., and Zisook, S. (1993). The course of normal grief. In M. Stroebe, W. Stroebe, and R. Hansson (Eds.), *Handbook of bereavement: Theory, research and intervention* (pp. 23-43). New York: Cambridge University Press.

Stevens, N. (1995). Gender and adaptation to widowhood in later life. *Ageing and Society,* 15(1), 37-58.

van den Hoonaard, D. K. (2001). *The widowed self: The older woman's journey through widowhood.* Ontario, Canada, Wilfrid Laurier University Press.

Vinick, B. H. (1978). Remarriage in old age. *The Family Coordinator,* 27, 359-363.

5

The Dilemma of Repartnering: Considerations of Older Men and Women Entering New Intimate Relationships in Later Life

Jenny de Jong Gierveld

The transition from marriage to widowhood is one that is broadly expected after the age of fifty, the more so for women in the higher age brackets. Additionally, more and more people are confronted with divorce after fifty years of age; the percentages are still low, but are rising (Cooney, 1993; National Institute of Statistics Belgium, 2000; United Nations, 2001). Given the increasing reluctance, all over the Western world, voluntarily to embark on co-residence with adult children (and grandchildren), these phenomena together result in increasing numbers of older adults living in one-person households. The majority of older people living alone are women (United Nations, 2000). Many older widows, widowers, and divorcees are still healthy and face a future that is characterized by an ever-increasing life expectancy. What are the options open to them, to guarantee a future that will be characterized by well-being? In this article I am particularly interested in investigating repartnering as one of the pathways older people can take to alleviate social isolation and loneliness. Is repartnering a helpful life-strategy in actively coping with the challenges of later life?

Author note: I would like to thank Annemarie Peeters and Angelo Somers for their assistance in the reinterviewing of repartnered respondents.

Our central research question can be formulated as: What do we know about widowed and divorced women and men aged fifty or over, and their pathways to new partner relationships? In cases where older women and men meet a potential new partner, are they opting for remarriage or are they choosing other pathways to realize companionship?

In the next section of this chapter the theoretical framework of this study will be addressed, followed by the outcomes of the research. The outcomes include several characteristics of repartnered older adults subdivided according to their type of living arrangements, based on the large NESTOR-LSN survey dataset described later. Additionally, the results of a qualitative study encompassing in-depth reinterviewing of forty-six of the repartnered respondents of the NESTOR-survey will be presented. A discussion section closes the chapter.

Repartnering at Ages Fifty and Over: Opportunities and Restrictions

A certain percentage of older adults, confronted with the prospect of living alone and the risk of becoming lonely, think about starting a new partner relationship. Ganong et al. (1998) point to the fact that in the United States about half a million people over the age of sixty-five remarry each year, and the number is likely to increase, because overall numbers of older people will rise.

Older adults' level of well-being is crucially determined by their living arrangements. Older people will be well aware of the possible negative consequences of *living alone*. Living alone means that companionship and solidarity, as well as assistance and care, has to come from outside the household. Living alone therefore increases the need to create and maintain an integrative and supportive social network of family members, friends, neighbors, colleagues, and acquaintances. In contrast, *living together as a couple* is the living arrangement that provides older men and women with the greatest possibilities for social integration. One's spouse can and will serve as the optimal (long-term) provider of emotional as well as instrumental support. Nearly all husbands and three-quarters of wives rely on their spouses (Kendig et al., 1999). Spouses have the proximity, the long-term commitment, and the similarity in interests and values that underpin this type of support (Dykstra, 1993).

All over the Western world, life expectancy of women exceeds life expectancy of men by several years, resulting in high percentages of widows and relatively low percentages of widowers in the higher age brackets. The majority of men remain married until death. This is in sharp contrast to the marital position of older women as they age. Given the bias in absolute numbers of older men and women confronted with the breakup of the partner relationship, the *opportunities and restrictions* for women and men in the partner market in later life differ accordingly. In this respect, men are in a much better position, and consequently, might prefer to find a new heterosexual partner in the younger age brackets.

On the other hand, it is to be expected that an important percentage of the older widowed and divorced women and men will *prefer* to continue to live alone. They might be guided by the conviction that "enough is enough." They have conscientiously and warmheartedly dedicated themselves towards all the responsibilities associated with their long-term conjugal roles. Perhaps they also cared for a sick husband or wife for many years and tended them until death. They may not contemplate repartnering. Having said that, it is not clear if all older adults who think about repartnering will choose remarriage or—perhaps—opt for more flexible bonds with a new partner. Research in several countries has indicated an increase in unmarried cohabitation among young adults, be it for a shorter or longer period of time before marriage, or as a long-term alternative to marriage. However, until now, there has been very little research investigating the ideas and attitudes of older people about the types of living arrangements to be made with a new partner. It is not yet known if elderly people who repartner start de facto flexible living arrangements such as unmarried cohabitation or Living Apart Together (LAT),[1] instead of remarriage.

It is imaginable that some older people who consider repartnering, *older women* in particular, will try to refrain from remarriage because of the burdens involved in this type of living arrangement. Becoming a widow may also have improved the lives of older women to a certain extent, as they have more or less "retired" from the often-heavy domestic and other responsibilities associated with the conjugal role. In the period following the death of their spouse, and after a period of intense bereavement and the difficult process of coping, older people may have found a new state of equilibrium, self-confidence and self-sufficiency (Bennett, 1997; Davidson, 2001). This new situation may involve good contacts with siblings, children, and other members of the social network and enjoying a certain degree of freedom and independence in organizing their daily life.

A certain percentage of older widowed and divorced women and men—refraining from remarriage—might be open to a flexible type of living arrangement to be realized with a new partner such as unmarried cohabitation (Wu and Balakrishnan, 1994) and LAT relationships. These people envisage more possibilities for an equal position of both partners in these types of living arrangements as well as better guaranteeing ongoing independence.

In meeting potential new partners, older widowed or divorced women and men have to weigh carefully the pros and cons of the situation to be expected against the situation in which they currently find themselves. On the one hand there is the intimacy of a new partner relationship with all its possibilities of companionship, sharing both good and bad times, and alleviating the risk of loneliness (especially during the weekends). On the other hand they need to envisage the risk of restrictions in independently deciding about their daily life, and being confronted with biases in the sharing of tasks and responsibilities.

Life-Strategies Guiding Choices Concerning Future Pathways

All the factors mentioned so far are concerned with directing the specific decisions to be made about future behavior. These factors will be viewed together as being part of people's more encompassing ideas about how their lives will evolve, in other words their life-strategies (Liefbroer, 1998). Giddens suggests that life planning constitutes a general feature of modern life:

> In a world of alternative lifestyle options, strategic life-planning becomes of special importance. ... Life-planning is a means of preparing a course of future actions mobilized in terms of the self's biography (1991: 85).

The concept of individual-level strategic behavior covers decision-making in a wide variety of domains of life, including—in my opinion—the domain of the start of a new partner relationship and the specific type of living arrangement to be chosen and realized with the new partner. Opting for flexible living arrangements after repartnering at an older age is to be considered an example of these hitherto under-recognized skills of older adults, although, as Ranzijn writes,

> the structures and attitudes of many sectors of society have not caught up with the reality of ageing, which is that, with relatively few exceptions, ... older people are vital, self-reliant and creatively involved with their communities (2002: 83).

Research Design

Data

Data have been taken from the NESTOR-Living Arrangements and Social Networks (LSN) survey (Knipscheer et al., 1995). Face-to-face interviews were conducted in 1992 with 4,494 men and women in the Netherlands aged fifty-five to eighty-nine years. The sample was stratified according to sex and year of birth. The same numbers of men and women were selected for each year of birth. In addition, the sample was selected in such a way that after five years, that is, at the end of the second wave of the longitudinal survey, the numbers of men and women in the oldest age categories would still be large enough to be studied. Names and addresses came from the registers of eleven municipalities in the Netherlands. The sample may be considered representative of the elderly population of the Netherlands (Broese van Groenou et al., 1995).

Respondents

From the respondents I selected the people who, after divorce or widowhood, have started a new partner relationship at the age of fifty or above (n=173). This group consists of forty-four women and 129 men.

In the questionnaire used in the NESTOR-LSN survey, using the principle of life histories, various details were requested about the start, the continuation, and the dissolution (through divorce or widowhood) of partner relationships. Included were marriages, but also unmarried cohabitation and LAT relationships. A network member was categorized as a partner if the respondents themselves explicitly classified this network member as a partner.

Starting in 1998 and continuing in 1999, a selection of forty-six respondents of the 1992 wave have been reinterviewed face-to-face and in-depth to determine—among other things—their motives and considerations for entering into a specific type of living arrangement after repartnering at the age of fifty or later. Among the forty-six interviews analyzed in this study, I conducted twenty-two with the LAT-ers; two trained students conducted twenty-four interviews, eleven with unmarried cohabiting older adults and thirteen with re-married people. The interview was mostly made up of open-ended questions. In this way in-depth information was gathered about the decision making process leading to a certain living arrangement, as well as about the preferences for sharing or not sharing finances and living arrangements.

Results

Quantitative Data Analyses: Survey 1992

Table 5.1 indicates descriptive characteristics of repartnered older women and men differentiated by current living arrangement: sixty-nine (40 percent) of the 173 repartnered older people have remarried. More than half of the repartnered older people have chosen a more flexible type of living arrangement: forty-eight (28 percent) started unmarried cohabitation and fifty-six (32 percent) a LAT relationship. In total, 13 percent of the older people available for repartnering have started a new partner relationship. The majority of the people who started a new partner relationship after fifty are male: 29 percent of the men and 5 percent of the older women repartnered. Demographic trends are responsible for this gender bias in repartnering. The data show that men are more heavily represented among the remarried and women among the people involved in a LAT relationship, although the relationship is not significant.

Taking partner history into account it becomes clear that divorcees form a significant percentage of all repartnered men and women. There is a tendency for divorcees to be more heavily represented among the remarried. Among people who started unmarried cohabitation or a LAT relationship, the widowed are certainly not negligible. However, the relationship is not significant. The majority of older repartnered people started the new partner relationship at ages between fifty and sixty-nine years. A relatively large percentage of LAT-ers, however, started the new partner relationship at ages seventy or above. This relationship is significant.

For the 173 respondents who repartnered after age fifty, differences in age between the two partners varied considerably, but for those remarried and for the LAT-ers mean differences are about twelve years, men being older. For those choosing unmarried cohabitation, the differences are more moderate.

Half of the older people who repartner take more than five years in between the two relationships. Further analysis (not shown explicitly in this chapter) indicates that men more frequently form a new partner relationship within a shorter period of time than do

Table 5.1

Characteristics of People in Different Types of Living Arrangements After Repartnering at Ages Fifty or over (%)

Characteristics	N	Remarried (n=69)	Unmarried Cohabitation (n=48)	LAT (n=56)
Men (n.s)	119	80	75	68
Women	44	20	25	32
Ever divorced? (n.s.)				
No	99	51	65	66
Yes	64	49	35	34
Age start final partner relation*				
50-69 yrs	122	86	74	56
70 yrs or more	41	14	26	44
Space between end former and start new partner relation (n.s.)				
Less than 5 yrs	82	47	55	51
5 yrs or more	81	53	45	49
Educational level (n.s.)				
6-10 yrs	107	57	71	70
11-18 yrs	56	43	29	30
Calender year at final repartnering**				
Until 1984	81	71	56	20
1985 or later	82	29	44	80

Note. Chi-square is significant with $^*p = .001$, and $^{**}p < .001$

women. An interval of more than ten years is especially characteristic of women who are involved in a LAT relationship. A relatively low level of education characterizes most of the older people as compared to younger generations. This phenomenon is reflected in the educational levels of the older repartnered: the majority had ten years' education or less. Although the more highly educated seemed to be more heavily involved in remarriage, the relationship is not significant.

Loneliness scores of the repartnered older adults turned out to be significantly lower than the scores for their peers who continued living alone. On the de Jong Gierveld loneliness scale (de Jong Gierveld and Kamphuis, 1985; de Jong Gierveld and van Tilburg, 1999) ranging from 0 (not lonely) to 11 (extremely lonely), the remarried had a mean of 2.9, the unmarried cohabiting 2.15, the LATers 2.16. In contrast those living alone had a mean score above the cutting point of three: 3.39. Repartnering proved to be positive in alleviating loneliness.

Finally, table 5.1 points out an interesting time effect. Repartnering women and men in the period before 1984 have chosen primarily to remarry. By far the majority of repartnering women and men after 1985 has chosen for LAT: this relationship is significant. Consequently, LAT is to be considered as a new, rapidly increasing phenomenon. What is it that directs older repartnering people towards refraining from remarriage, and choosing for a more flexible type of living arrangement?

In table 5.2 the results of a multivariate analysis on the determinants of choosing remarriage or one of the more flexible living arrangements after repartnering at an older age are presented. A hierarchical logistic regression analysis has been used. In the first step, five determinants are included. In the second step, the calendar year at final repartnering is added.

Step 1 shows that the differences registered in the bivariate analysis of table 5.1 remain significant in the multivariate analysis. A younger age at the start of the final partner relationship is significantly related to remarriage. An age of seventy or above is significantly related to attaining flexible living arrangements, after controlling for all the other variables. Less significant differences are found for gender and educational level of the respondents.

In step 2 of the hierarchical regression analysis, that is, after including the variable calendar year at final repartnering, this final variable proved to be the only one significantly and negatively related to remarriage after repartnering at an older age. Older repartnering people before 1985 have attained remarriage; older people after 1985 have had a greater probability of achieving flexible types of living arrangements. Age at the start of the latest partner relationship is no longer significantly related to the type of living arrangement achieved.

Table 5.2

Summary of Hierarchical Logistic Regression Analysis for Variables Predicting Remarriage versus Unmarried Cohabitation and LAT after Repartnering at Ages Fifty or over (n=163)

	B	SE B	β
Step 1			
Men (ref.)			
Women	-0.53	0.40	0.59+
Ever divorced?			
No (ref.)			
Yes	0.05	0.36	1.05
Age start final partner relation			
50-69 yrs (ref.)			
70 yrs or more	-1.16	0.45	0.31**
Space between end former and start new partner relation			
Less than 5 yrs (ref.)			
5 yrs or more	0.31	0.35	1.36
Educational level			
6-10 yrs (ref.)			
11-18 yrs	0.51	0.36	1.66+
Step 2			
Men (ref.)			
Women	-0.41	0.42	0.66
Ever divorced?			
No (ref.)			
Yes	0.02	0.38	1.02
Age start final partner relation			
50-69 yrs (ref.)			
70 yrs or more	-0.74	0.48	0.48+
Space between end former and start new partner relation			
Less than 5 yrs (ref.)			
5 yrs or more	0.54	0.37	1.71+
Educational level			
6-10 yrs (ref.)			
11-18 yrs	0.52	0.38	1.69+
Calender year at final repartnering			
Until 1984 (ref.)			
1985 or later	-1.39	0.37	0.24***

Note. Step 1, Cox & Snell $R^2 = 8.9\%$. Step 2, Cox & Snell $R^2 = 17.0\%$.
+$p < .18$, ** $p < .01$, *** $p < .001$

The outcomes of the second step of the multivariate analysis further suggest—to a certain extent and not significantly—that the people with shorter intervals between the end of the former and the start of the current partner relationship, and respondents in the lower-educated sectors of society—are confronted with a greater probability of achieving a flexible living arrangement at repartnering as compared to remarriage. Gender and partner history (being ever divorced, yes/no) are not significantly related to either the probability of remarriage or of achieving flexible types of living arrangements.

I repeat the question: what is it, what mechanisms, direct older repartnering people today away from remarriage and towards other living arrangements? I will now turn to the outcomes of the open interviews to elicit additional information on these questions.

Qualitative Data Analysis: The Results of In-Depth Reinterviewing 1998/1999

Respondents involved in the round of in-depth interviewing have among other things been asked, "What have been your most important reasons for opting for this type of living arrangement?" All respondents answered very quickly and convincingly, needing no time to think about their answers. In this chapter I will concentrate first on motives related to push factors such as avoiding or combating loneliness (de Jong Gierveld, 1998). Second, I will illustrate the motives and intentions of elderly people opting for remarriage, and of those not choosing this type of living arrangement at repartnering. Financial motives proved to be important factors in decision-making, and these motives will also be addressed.

Push Factors: Loneliness-Related Considerations Trigger Elderly People to Start a New Partner Relationship.

Man, eighty years, LAT relationship

I know many elderly people who start a LAT relationship, simply for the sake of companionship. Most of them drink a cup of coffee together, share meals ... to avoid feeling lonely. Weekends are awful for people who live alone.

Man, seventy-three years, unmarried cohabitation

And I'd say to anyone who has been left on his own: go out and find yourself a nice lady friend to live with as quickly as you can!

Woman, sixty-eight years, unmarried cohabitation

Interviewer: what was/is the most important motive for going to live with him as a non-married person?

It wasn't a motive for me, it was for him ... he kept on nagging about it.

Interviewer: and then you acted positively?

Yes, stupidly enough ... feeling sorry for someone, I think ... efface yourself a little. ...

Because for men when they are alone, I think ... in my opinion, it's always more difficult than for a woman, a woman can support herself much more.

Interviewer: How long were you widowed before this man came into your life?

Two years, but it never was my intention to get a man. But perseverance pays ... He (her first husband) did say on his sickbed you mustn't remain alone, so in a way he gave his permission.

Interviewer: But you could very well manage on your own?

Yes, very well indeed.

Man, seventy-two years, unmarried cohabitation

Interviewer: what was/is the most important reason for you to start unmarried cohabitation?

Interviewee [starts laughing] I did not have a motive at all. ... After the death of my first wife, ... she died soon after our divorce ... I had a lot of self-confidence, I said to myself, I will stay alone, be single, and I will frequent a restaurant, I will look for companionship. ... Then I met her, and firstly I did not want to be involved with this woman ... all the problems, but then all of a sudden I thought ... maybe it's better that I give her the money that I intended to use in the restaurant ... then I give her some help, and moreover it's much more fun for me. ... You have a bit of companionship, just talk a little bit about the daily things and, and, that's what you need if you live all alone, otherwise you become shy and inward looking, you will end up as an awfully difficult person ... and so it happened, yes ... at her age, she so young and with two young kids, and then me ... I just let go ... and it happened to be great ... yes, still great, taking into account my age. Great!!

Pull Factors: Religious Values or Traditional Ideas about the Bonds Between the Partners Influence the Decision in Favor of Remarriage.

Several respondents mentioned explicitly that living arrangements other than remarriage after repartnering would be unthinkable for them. Remarriage is the living arrangement that has been broadly socially accepted for centuries, both in the religious and other more traditional sectors of society. One of the respondents formulated his ideas as follows:

Man, eighty-two years, remarried

Interviewer: what was the reason that you married her?

Yeah, I loved her and I was alone. My first wife died in 1981.

Interviewer: did you cohabit with her before you remarried?

No!

Interviewer: what kind of relationship do you have, can you tell me something about that?

The ideas, our thinking was on a similar level. Yes, also religiously and that is very important. Living together and being not married, I disapprove of it deep in my heart. These things happen nowadays, but I do condemn.

Pull Factors: Strong Feelings of Independence and Autonomy Influence the Choice of Flexible Living Arrangements.

Woman, seventy-one years, LAT relationship

Interviewer: how would you describe the bond between you and your partner?

Very strong, but do not wish to live with forever. We both have our own lives.

[She describes her partner as a rather dominant man. She has been a widow for over nine years and is used to living her own life.]

Since we both have a life behind us ... it's much more difficult than starting from scratch ... He is an authoritarian type of person. ... He is always trying to fix things for me.

Woman, eighty-four years, LAT relationship

Interviewer: but now I have some important questions: now you have been around together a great deal, you are going to him, he is coming over here, but you continue to live independently? You are not thinking of living together? Why?

No, that's not what I want to do, for that we are both too stubborn. I believe it wouldn't work if we were together everyday and for 24 hours. And he always gets up so early in the morning! And he is always very busy; I can't take that anymore, that's too much for me. And when I have been there and have been helping him with all kinds of things, then I'm always glad that I can stay in bed until 9.00 in the morning *[laughing]*. He often says, "You can also stay in bed here," but I don't want that.

I find older people very stupid when they do that, they give up their houses and are going to live together, but what if it doesn't work out, what will happen then?

Woman, eight-five years, LAT relationship

Interviewer: so, you were doing all kinds of things together, but you never thought about living together? Why not?

We didn't want that because we have freedom, you know ... when you live alone and if you want to go you can go when you want. And ... because I have many friends, and I have learned to play bridge.

Interviewer: and he? Men want to ... what did he think about it? Did he want to ...?

Well ... he couldn't do this anymore.

Interviewer: but in the beginning, when he could do this, didn't he say then ...?

No, from the beginning I said ...

Interviewer: you said, "I want to keep my freedom!"

Yes!

Pull Factors: Financial Considerations Direct Older People to Remarriage, Unmarried Cohabitation, or Living Apart Together.

The strategic behavior of older people is also influenced by financial considerations. Several of the respondents mentioned explicitly that they have chosen certain pathways to optimize their overall (future) financial position and that of their partner. All Dutch residents aged sixty-five and over are entitled to a basic state pension that allows them to continue living privately in their family homes and neighborhood at above poverty level. Hence the need for financial security rarely forms in itself the stimulus to repartner. In repartnering, however, the choice of either remarriage or another type of living arrangement can have positive or negative effects on the availability of additional private pension schemes (for those aged sixty-five and over) or on social security entitlements (for those of younger age groups).

Man, sixty-three years, remarried

Interviewer: why did you remarry?

Very materialistically, then .... it had to do with my partner ... I had built up a good pension, but our pension fund will not yet accept, allow that ... a not married partner claims rights to the late husband's pension, so it really had to do with very materialistic...

Man, sixty-two years, LAT

We did not aim at living together because of our freedom, and ... in that case we lose our social security benefits.

Man, eight-five years, (unregistered) unmarried cohabitation, and his partner

Look, both of us have the full AOW *[the state pension allowance]*[2] and when you marry, they take part of the AOW. We have been thinking about it, but you will have less ...

[Partner adds]: But in that case we are hundreds of guilders worse off per month, and they will stop my rent subsidizing, and then we have to pay everything ourselves. We talked a lot about it, but we did not figure out, calculate exactly. ... When I am obliged to marry, ok, I will do so, but we have said, why marry? ... We lose so much and we can't afford that. That's the kernel, we lose too much, much too much money.

Man, eighty-four years, LAT

I prefer to be independent. ... I have one daughter ... and, yes, some money, and she has more children and no money. ... A marriage would soon bring us problems. I do prefer to give my money to my daughter and my grandchildren.

Discussion

Given the increase in elderly people living alone, and a future that is characterized by an ever-increasing life expectancy, this chapter has aimed to investigate repartnering as one of the pathways that elderly people can take to alleviate social isolation and loneliness. Based on a representative sample of 4,494 men and women aged fifty-five to eighty-nine years, I selected the 173 respondents who repartnered after the age of fifty. The respondents were classified according to living arrangements attained at repartnering: remarriage, unmarried cohabitation, or Living Apart Together. Survey data about the 173 respondents as well as the data of in-depth re-interviewing of forty-six of these older adults have been presented in this chapter.

In older age, the opportunities and restrictions to begin a new partner relationship after widowhood or divorce are by-and-large dependent on the demographic characteristics of the elderly people. Due to gender differences in life expectancy, the majority of the very old are women and the percentage of widows is much higher than the percentage of widowers in the oldest age brackets. Most widowed older people live in one-person households. In contrast to the situation in the past, adults aged sixty-five years and older in the Netherlands can today rely on state pension schemes that allow them to live financially independently in their own homes. Consequently, there is no direct financial motive that forces them to repartner.

However, living alone in older age can produce feelings of loneliness. In order to alleviate loneliness and given the extra number of years to be spent in good health, elderly people might 'opt' for new partner relationships. If elderly people are successful in finding a new partner, they have to decide—among other things—about the living arrangements to be selected at repartnering.

Remarriage following widowhood is the arrangement that has received widespread cultural approval over the centuries. After remarriage the social, cultural, and legal characteristics of the new living arrangements are well known to everyone in the family and community. Remarried men and women share living quarters and finances. Other financial consequences of remarriage (for example, inheritance) are fixed as well, following legal administrative rules. So, remarriage offers security and familiarity. Additionally, in cases where one of the spouses is confronted with long-term illness or handicap, the other spouse will function as the first care provider.

Compared to remarriage, unmarried cohabitation is a living arrangement characterized by more uncertainties about financial and familial rights. In general non-household members do not know if finances are shared, and if pension schemes include both partners. Will the late partner be allowed to continue living in the formerly shared living quarters? What about inheritance? Do children have to 'wait' for the new partner's death to sell the parental home? Are the new partners both accepted as part of the family-at-large and are both invited to family gatherings?

Those attaining LAT after repartnering are, to a large extent, characterized by continuation of the situation "living alone." These older adults continue to live in their former family homes, even if it is on a part-time basis. Children and grandchildren who used to visit the older parent in this house can continue to do so, and in doing so will participate in all the minutiae of the atmosphere of the parental home (father's chair and mother's pots and pans), still available. On a part-time basis the new partners share accommodation, providing both of them with companionship, solidarity, and intimacy. For children and other network members this situation is totally transparent: neither finances nor living quarters are legally shared. This includes open opportunities after bereavement for children to decide about the parental belongings. Whether or not the LAT partner will be accepted by children and other social network members as part of the family-at-large is dependent on many factors.

Sharing living quarters on a twenty-four-hour basis, whether the partners are married or not, presupposes that both will have to adapt to the new situation, with new "rules" and "household habits." As far as social well-being and loneliness is concerned, it is known also from this study that mean loneliness scores of the repartnered are significantly lower than loneliness scores of those continuing to live alone. However, the intensity of familial integration with children and siblings of the repartnered lags behind those of the parents living alone (de Jong Gierveld and Peeters, 2003).

We have to conclude that LAT relationships in general offer better opportunities to continue life as usual, and to optimize family integration and social networking than repartnering and sharing living quarters on a twenty-four-hour basis. Given these evaluations of the pros and cons of different living arrangements it will come as no surprise that our data indicate that older adults today are open to new intimate relationships after widowhood or divorce, but that they hesitate to remarry and hesitate to reenter into a two-person household. In total, 40 percent of those repartnered after age fifty remarried and 60 percent attained a more flexible living arrangement. The older person fears the problems involved in a twenty-four-hour personal relationship with a new partner. This is the more so in cases of people aged seventy and over: among those over seventy years of age, a relatively large percentage attained a LAT relationship, indicating a broad acceptance and willingness to achieve this less socially, culturally and legally fixed type of living arrangement. Women were notably explicit and detailed in formulating their considerations in this context. One of them formulated this dilemma as follows: "After a period of living alone, you have fixed habits. ... It is difficult to adjust. ... If you are very old, you are a whole person, and it is difficult to change your habits."

This finding is in line with the interview results of Pyke (1994) that a relatively high percentage of women move away from a male-dominated first marriage towards a power-sharing type of repartnering. Women have shown their ability to survive on their own financially and emotionally after bereavement or divorce. Their increased self-confidence and self-sufficiency have greatly increased not only their power in the repartnering market, but also their reluctance to remarry and their power to negotiate alternative living arrangements.

To a certain extent this research outcome is in line with what has been found by Henry and Lovelace (1995), that repartnering as such is a stressful event. It is stressful because many changes have to be faced. The older the new partners, the more problems have to be faced in leaving behind old behavioral patterns and habits and establishing and accepting new ones. New partner bonds at older ages involve, by definition, two people, both of whom are characterized by specific life histories and have evolved into people with unique personalities and lifelong personality traits. Can these personalities still be patterned, remodeled, and harmonized as they could at young ages? Achieving a LAT relationship should be relatively less stressful. In particular, the latter option provides the opportunity to relax in one's own home from time to time, and in doing so take a period of "distance from the new partner," to be better and freshly prepared to enjoy time together. Apparently, the extra burdens of traveling and of continuing the maintenance and cleaning of two living quarters do not function as a barrier to achieving well-being in LAT relationships.

The in-depth interviews with people involved in a LAT relationship showed that for older widows, widowers, and divorcees, the strong desire to continue living in the familiar setting of their family homes and being able to make independent decisions about their day-to-day activities, in combination with a desire to share time with a partner to avoid loneliness and to be comforted by mutual solidarity, has led them to start a LAT relationship. In doing this, they are realizing the benefits of combining a partner relationship with a one-person household.

Our data did not allow us to investigate the provision of care after repartnering. Only one of the interviewees mentioned care taking, especially the risk of caring for another sick partner, explicitly as a point of consideration and discussions at the start of the new partner relationship (Man, eighty-five years, LAT): *"From the start we agreed that if anyone of us will be wrecked, then it's over.... At our age it's impossible to care for a sick partner."*

Further research is needed to elicit the long-term quality and mutual support between the two partners, differentiated according to types of living arrangements.

The statements of elderly people about the financial aspects of repartnering indicate that a majority of them fear ending up in a situation where they will be financially worse off. Hence, financial considerations proved to be very influential in selecting the optimal living arrangement when repartnering at an older age. For elderly people with low levels of private pensions, the expected loss at remarriage of the late husband's private pension for the widow is a strong trigger towards avoiding remarriage. Well-to-do respondents, however, have more opportunities to achieve remarriage, because the expected financial loss to the widow is acceptable and can be "absorbed." Others consciously opt for remarriage. This is especially so in cases where the repartnering women have no (or very low) personal private pension entitlements. Remarriage secures a survivor's pension after the death of a new spouse. In future research we need to know more about the financial situation (income and pension entitlements) of both partners before repartnering, as well as data that will allow weighing the financial motives against other considerations. New research is needed as a means of furthering understanding of the repartnering processes in later life.

Notes

1. A LAT relationship is defined as a partner relationship in which the partners continue to live in their own houses/apartments, and intermittently share households, be it during the weekends or otherwise.
2. The state pension scheme allows both partners of a married or cohabiting couple 70 percent of the allowance for an elderly men or women living in a one-person household.

References

Bennett, K. M. (1997). A longitudinal study of well-being in widowed women. *International Journal of Geriatric Psychiatry*, 12: 61-66.

Broese van Groenou, M. I., van Tilburg, T. G., de Leeuw, E. D., and Liefbroer, A. C. (1995). Data collection. In C. P. M. Knipscheer, J. de Jong Gierveld, T. G. van Tilburg, and P. A. Dykstra (Eds.), *Living arrangements and social networks of older adults* (pp. 185-197). Amsterdam, the Netherlands: VU University Press.

Cooney, T. M. (1993). Recent demographic change: implications for families planning for the future. *Marriage and Family Review*, 18 (3/4), 37-55.

Davidson, K. (2001). Reconstructing life after a death: Psychological adaptation and social role transition in the medium and long term for older widowed men and women in the UK. *Indian Journal of Gerontology*, 15(1-2): 221-136.

de Jong Gierveld, J. (1998). A review of loneliness: Concept and definitions, determinants and consequences. *Reviews in Clinical Gerontology*, 8, 73-80.
de Jong Gierveld, J. and Kamphuis, F. H. (1985). The development of a Rasch-type loneliness scale. *Applied Psychological Measurement*, 9, 289-299.
de Jong Gierveld, J. and Peeters, A. (2003). The interweaving of repartnered older adults' lives with their children and siblings: How this relates to standard and new types of living arrangements. *Ageing and Society* 23, 187-205.
de Jong Gierveld, J. and van Tilburg, T. G. (1999). *Manual of the Loneliness Scale.* Amsterdam, the Netherlands: Vrije University, Department of Social Research Methodology.
Dykstra, P. A. (1993). The differential availability of relationships and the provision and effectiveness of support to older adults. *Journal of Social and Personal Relationships*, 10, 355-370.
Ganong, L., Coleman, M., McDaniel, A. K., and Killian, T. (1998). Attitudes regarding obligations to assist an older parent or stepparent following later-life remarriage. *Journal of Marriage and the Family*, 60, 595-610.
Giddens, A. (1991). *Modernity and self-identity: Self and society in the late modern age.* Cambridge, UK: Polity Press.
Henry, C. S., and Lovelace, S. G. (1995). Family resources and adolescent family life satisfaction in remarried family households. *Journal of Family Issues*, 16, 765-786.
Kendig, H., Koyano, W., Asakawa, T., and Ando, T. (1999). Social support of older people in Australia and Japan. *Ageing and Society*, 19, 185-208.
Knipscheer, C. P. M., de Jong Gierveld, J., van Tilburg, T. G., and Dykstra, P. A. (1995). *Living arrangements and social networks of older adults.* Amsterdam, the Netherlands: VU University Press.
Liefbroer, A. C. (1998). *Studying family formation and dissolution from a macro-perspective: Temporal patterns and their relation to economic growth.* Paper presented at the workshop on 'Transition into Adulthood,' Brussels, Belgium.
National Institute of Statistics Belgium. (2000). *Bevolkingsstatistieken: Huwelijken en Echtscheidingen in 1999* [Population Statistics: Marriage and Divorce in 1999]. Brussels, Belgium.
Pyke, K. D. (1994). Women´s employment as gift or burden? Marital power across marriage, divorce, and remarriage. *Gender and Society*, 8 (1), 73-91.
Ranzijn, R. (2002). Towards a positive psychology of ageing: Potentials and barriers. *Australian Psychologist*, 37 (2), 79-85.
United Nations. (2000). *Women and men in Europe and North America.* New York/Geneva, Switzerland: United Nations Publications.
United Nations. (2001). *United Nations Historical Dataset 1950-1990.* New York: United Nations Publications.
Wu, Z., and Balakrishnan, T. R. (1994). Cohabitation after marital disruption in Canada. *Journal of Marriage and the Family*, 56, 723-734.

6

Attitudes of Older Widows and Widowers in New Brunswick, Canada towards New Partnerships

Deborah Kestin van den Hoonaard

"*Marry in haste; repent at leisure.*" Is there any doubt that the widow who shared this sentiment with me felt that the preferable and safer thing to do after losing a spouse is to remain single? It is "common knowledge" in Canada that older women who become widowed are unlikely to remarry while men are both more likely to marry and to marry quickly, too quickly some would say. This article looks primarily at the first part of the equation, widows' attitudes towards remarriage and relationships with men.

The data for this paper come from a qualitative study that examined the social meaning of widowhood from the perspective of the women who experienced it. There were three parts to the study: in-depth interviews with twenty-eight women in New Brunswick, Canada ranging in age from fifty-three to eighty-seven who had been widowed within the previous five years; observation of a six-week workshop, "Striving on Your Own," put on by the Third Age Centre, a partner in the research; and a focus group of ten widows who examined a summary of the findings and commented on them. Further work is currently being conducted with widowers, of whom

---

Author note: The study on which this paper is based was funded by a Community Researcher Award given by the Seniors' Independence Research Program of Health Canada (NHRDP award no. 6604-111-603). The Third Age Centre at St. Thomas University, Fredericton, New Brunswick, Canada, was a partner in the research.

twenty-one have to date been interviewed, and preliminary results are given later.

New Brunswick is a small, culturally conservative, and religious Maritime province in Atlantic Canada. Although there are a few small cities, New Brunswick is essentially a rural province comprised almost entirely of forests. Its population is quite homogeneous—primarily descendants of immigrants from the United Kingdom, and includes a proud group of Loyalists and Acadians. New Brunswick is the only officially bilingual province in Canada. About 40 percent of its population is francophone, many of whom live in the northern part. There are also several First-Nations Reserves. The religious composition of the province is overwhelmingly Protestant and Catholic, and church parking lots are often full on Sundays.

The interviews with the widowed women included open and broad questions in order to encourage them to frame their stories in their own way. They averaged two hours in duration, and the women showed strong emotions from time to time although none declined to discuss an issue. With only a few exceptions, the women did not bring up the issue of remarriage, repartnering, or men until I did. This is in stark contrast to the men who have participated in a current study of men's experiences as widowers.[1] The men often brought up the issue of women and repartnering or marriage in response to the very first question of the interview that simply asked them to talk about their experience as widowers without specifying any particular issues.

All of the women who volunteered to participate in the study on which this chapter is based were single at the time of the interview although at least two have since married. There would be different results had remarried women volunteered, particularly because so few participants expressed any desire to repartner.

Widows represent a significant portion of the over-sixty-five female population of Canada. Forty-seven percent of women in this age group are widows, and this percentage rises to 79 percent in the eighty-five-and-over age group. In contrast, only 13 percent of men over sixty-five are widowers, and this percentage increases to only 39 percent for the eighty-five-and-over group, in which 51 percent of men are still married (Elliot et al., 1996: 18). In addition, for the sixty-five-and-over group, there are seventy-two men for every 100 women and only forty-four for every woman in the eighty-five-and-older age group (ibid: 14). In 2001, New Brunswick had 34,468 widows compared to 7,111 widowers, resulting in a ratio of 4.8 widows for every widower (Statistics Canada, 2001). These figures communicate the significantly skewed availability of potential partners for women versus men. Thus, even if half of women were uninterested in remarriage or other repartnering, there are likely still enough women who do want a relationship with a man for a widower to find a new wife relatively easily. Some men might even feel they need to be wary of "predatory" women.

Attitudes towards Remarriage

Not surprisingly, most of the women who participated in the study, fifteen out of twenty-three who expressed a preference, were not interested in remarriage or in a romantic relationship with another man. The most common reason is that they believe they have already had the best possible husband and would find themselves comparing a second husband to their first: *"It would be completely unfair. I'd be comparing all the time."*[2]

Indeed, several women's ideas about their husbands would qualify for Lopata's notion of "husband sanctification" (1981). This process of sanctification results in women developing "an extremely idealized image of their husbands" and of their marital relationship (Lopata, 1996: 117). One woman went so far as to describe her husband as a *"perfect man."*

Peg felt that she would not only be comparing two men but also two times of life. Nothing could approach her *"young, romantic marriage."* She believed that a new man would be unlikely to bring her *"flowers and things like that."* Nostalgia pervades her memory of her marriage and her courtship experience during the Blitz when her husband had *"saved my life, really."* Who could compete with such recollections?

Another reason for not wanting to remarry is a sense of already having suffered enough. A few women were widowed for the second time, and others had spent a long time enduring their husbands' illnesses and caring for them. They made comments like, *"I don't want to go through that again, and [I'd] rather be alone than go through all that agony again"* (Marilyn, early sixties).

Sylvia, who had lost two husbands, both suddenly, felt that she could not take another loss on that scale.

Third, some women acknowledged that, although they did not regret the relationship they had with their husbands, they had compromised or scheduled their lives around their husbands. These women did not care to repeat this pattern with someone else, particularly because they have gotten used to being in charge of their own lives: *"I'm quite contented the way I am. I am my own boss here and [can] come and go as I please"* (Sharon, mid-sixties).

Most of the widows had lived in "traditional" marriages and had taken primary responsibility for household upkeep. Lucy, for example, noted that she had *"catered"* to her husband while Marion had been unable to listen to the kind of music she liked because her husband preferred a different type. Although several women felt that marriages were happier when gender roles were more clearly defined than they are today, they were not willing to repeat the traditional pattern with someone new, and a couple commented that men who wanted to marry were probably *"looking for someone to look after them."*

Finally, their deep attachment to their husbands influenced a few women's attitudes about possible remarriage. Three went so far as to comment that they felt they were *"still married."* Only one woman noted that her husband had exacted a promise from her that she not remarry. It is noteworthy that she did not feel that this promise was unreasonable and had every intention of following his wishes.

Wedding Rings

Based on their sentiments regarding remarriage, it is not surprising that most of the participants still wore their wedding rings. When I commented on this fact, simply saying something like, "I see you still wear your wedding ring," the most common response was that they had no intention of marrying again. These women obviously interpreted the removal of their rings as an indication of willingness and interest in remarriage. For example, when I asked Lucy if she would wear her rings for the rest of her life, she commented: *"Oh no, I won't touch them. I have no interest in ever getting married again"* (Lucy, early seventies).

The ring has come to symbolize not only the desire to remain single, but it also helps the women maintain a sense of closeness with their husbands. Some women said they would *"wear it forever"* and would feel terrible if they ever had to take it off. Illness forced Emily to have her ring removed, and she had been concerned that acquaintances might interpret its absence as disloyalty and/or interest in another man. She remarked: *"I had to go to a stranger. I couldn't go to anybody I knew"* (Emily, sixty-five).

I had first become interested in the importance of wedding rings when reading *Widow* (Caine 1974), a published autobiographical account of Lynn Caine's experience with losing her husband. Caine reports that, in a moment of anger at her loss, she threw her wedding ring out of the window of a cab in New York City and then spent the following day fruitlessly trying to find it. Two of the women in this study had had to remove their rings for health reasons, and their description of the experience communicated a comparable sense of distress. In contrast, two of the four women who had voluntarily removed their wedding rings have remarried.[3]

Wedding rings also serve as a protection against unwanted attention from men. They prevent them from knowing that a woman is a widow or thinking that she is interested in a romantic relationship:

> Well, suppose someone else comes along, if a man comes along and sees you have your wedding band, he's not going to approach you *(Eileen, early sixties)*.

> I don't think there'd be any use of letting people know I was available *(Frances, eighty-seven)*.

Although the majority of women were clear that they did not find the decision to keep their ring on a difficult one, there was some ambiguity surrounding the issue. One woman asked me what I thought she should do while others reported that people had commented to them that they should remove their rings.

Eleanor's situation illustrates the dilemma some women encounter. She was willing to remarry and took off her wedding ring when she was going out with a man because, *"I felt he would be embarrassed."* She was not entirely comfortable with the decision and does sometimes still wear her ring. This woman's son was upset that she had removed her wedding ring, and this was a dilemma for her: *"And then I think, 'Why do I have to make excuses for my children?'"*

In the end, Eleanor decided to keep her ring off in order to make her male friend more comfortable, but she, too, recognized that she had to deal with the symbol of the ring as an indication of loyalty to her husband, for she noted: *"It doesn't change how much I loved [my husband ... [But] we can pick up the pieces and make a life, or we can wallow in it and be miserable and make everybody else miserable"* (Eleanor, late fifties).

Clearly, this woman's experience and understanding reflect the complex issues surrounding what might otherwise appear to be a simple decision, whether or not to wear one's wedding ring once widowed.

Cautionary Tales about Second Marriages

Whether or not individual women want to get married again, widows seem to agree that remarriage can be a risky business. Several recounted second-marriage horror stories that may be characterized as "cautionary tales" (Hochschild, 1989). These stories include the common elements of a second marriage that takes place too quickly, disastrous consequences that are sometimes ironic (for example, when a woman's husband dies of cancer and then her second husband is diagnosed with cancer almost immediately following the marriage), and two unhappy families: *"I guess I saw A's sister, she got married the second time, and it was devastating ... a lot of hardship because you have two families ... [Second marriages] are harder"* (Sharon, mid-sixties).

In another example, a man *"flew"* into a second marriage only to find out that his new wife was manic-depressive. The pervasiveness of these stories underlines the general feeling of uncertainty surrounding taking a chance on remarriage.

Negotiating Relationships with Men

Although the participants were generally not interested in becoming romantically involved, some women did want male company whether for companionship or for physical, albeit not intimate, contact. Consistent with observations in Davidson (1999), several women expressed a desire to have someone to go out with or to be with when out. June, for example, likes to go ballroom dancing. She commented: *"Just to go out for dinner ... and dancing for a few hours ... and then you just go home and you've had a lovely evening and look at my husband's picture up there on the wall and I think it's a nice night's adventure"* (June, early seventies).

June especially likes ballroom studios, where it is understood that your partner is only your partner for dancing and no further relationship is expected.

Other women like the conversation of men but were concerned that a man with whom they attempted to be friends would misread their intentions and think: *"You're looking for a husband, and* *that's not necessarily it, it's nice just to have a frien*d" (Audrey, mid-fifties).

Marion remarked that you have to be wary if you do something domestic, for example, "*If you bake bread ... they get all nervous. And I just think it's nice to do something for people ... I have to be very careful not to overwhelm them*" (Marion, late fifties).

Both men and women often think that a cross-gender friendship implies romance, courtship and an intimate sexual relationship (Adams, 1985; Wright, 1991), and this belief constrains some women from making any attempt to have contact with men at all.

Several women noted that they enjoy physical contact with men, but they were not interested in an intimate relationship. These women were very creative in finding safe avenues for such contact, primarily hugging, in environments where it could not be misconstrued as an overture to a more intimate relationship. Martha and Sharon, for example, relied on particular men at their church for hugs. The safety of the Sunday service was underlined for both women by the fact that these hugs took place in the presence of these men's wives and were so obviously harmless that nobody found them a threat. Sharon explains: "*Like B. and I, we'd never think anything of it. We'd start hugging each other up [at church], but [his wife] is such a sweetheart*" (Sharon, mid-sixties).

Only three women, all in their fifties, spoke of missing sexual intimacy. Audrey, who has since remarried, explained: "*Even the sex thing, I mean, I found that hard, really lonely ... sexual desire... and no way of fulfilling that*" (Audrey, mid-fifties).

June's husband had died of Alzheimer's Disease, and she had been faithful to her husband during the extended time they had not had a sexual relationship because of his illness. She said that she: "*Didn't miss that ... like some women might if their husband just died suddenly. Because I didn't have it for so long*" (June, early seventies).[4]

For the few women who were interested in an intimate relationship, the changing mores regarding sex provided a challenge. Going out with a man on a date for the first time in twenty, thirty, or forty years could be "*traumatizing.*" Marion and Audrey both likened it to feeling like a teenager again "*at the beginning of some sort of physical relationship.*" When these women were growing up, intimate relationships were, for the most part, confined to marriage. They are well aware that things have changed considerably in this area, and a couple of participants were almost apologetic about their "*outdated*" moral standards. Nonetheless, they were not about to "*crawl into bed with somebody*" because "*there has to be a relationship*" (Eleanor, late fifties).

The participants recognized that men might not share their reluctance to engage in casual sexual relationships, and this recognition added another impediment to their being willing to go out with men. This concern was not necessarily unwarranted, as attested to by Edith, who had gone out to dinner with someone thinking that they were just going to "*go out and talk.*" The man she was with expected her to: "*Go around with him, go away with him and all that. You wouldn't imagine that at our age, but he did*" (Edith, early seventies).

Although some of the widows that I interviewed in a Florida retirement community were not averse to living together without getting married (van den Hoonaard, 1994), the widows who participated in the Canadian study did not see it as an option. The conservative moral climate in New Brunswick is a factor, and I came across virtually no LAT relationships among the widows.[5]

Another barrier to both friendships and couple relationships with men was a worry about gossip. Some women were careful to arrange their contact with men with this in mind. For example, Peg has "*very strict rules*" about when male visitors leave her house in the evening because she lives in a small town where others might notice and jump to conclusions about late-night visitors. Dorothy, who had a non-romantic friendship with a widower, reported that a friend had warned her not to have the minister visit her in her home because of the impression it would make. She and the minister laughed about it, but the friend had not been joking. Audrey commented that in her small city: "*If you showed up at the market on Saturday morning, it means you slept together Friday night*" (Audrey, mid-fifties).

The widows knew about the dangers of their actions being misunderstood, and they also found the motives of men problematic and subject to confusion. Two contrasting stories highlight this problem. First, Audrey told me about being called by a man who had seen her at the cemetery when she was visiting her husband's grave. He had been visiting his wife's grave and was interested in getting together. Audrey commented that "*He's hurting and he's lonely ... I'm not going to encourage anything here*" (Audrey, mid-fifties). Her interpretation of his intentions seems to be correct.

Marilyn, on the other hand, also received attention from a man who had noticed her at the cemetery. Her reaction was similar to Audrey's. But in Marilyn's case, the man told her he was calling to warn her about some young men who were drinking beer when he was in the area the night before. She remarked: "*I immediately jumped to the conclusion he was going to come there and meet me the next night ... and I thought, 'Isn't it a riot that you jump to these conclusions'*" (Marilyn, early sixties).

Both women felt vulnerable and uncertain because they were interacting with men on a new basis, that of a single woman. They both jumped to conclusions about the men's intentions, one perhaps inferring his intentions correctly and the other perhaps incorrectly.

Getting Together

Although most of the women who participated in the study had no interest in developing significant relationships with men, there were three women who did report having a meaningful relationship. In these three cases, the women brought up aspects of their relationships many times during our interview in response to a variety of questions several of which would seem unconnected to that topic.

Audrey was at the point of having to make a decision about marriage.[6] The situation was challenging because her male friend has "*emotional baggage*" and because of others' resistance to their being a couple. Her story is strikingly different from a young woman's who would be looking toward a first marriage with innocent excitement. Rather she was concerned with divorce and AIDS, as well as the cautionary tales she had heard about second marriages.

Eleanor, who also thought she might someday marry, was involved with a slightly younger man who had never been married. The relationship dominated her thoughts so much that almost any question I asked led back to a discussion of their relationship and its potential to grow into something permanent. She felt that she and her friend experienced both well-meaning and hostile attention, including matchmaking, gossip and the hostility of her children to her seeing this man so steadily:

Our best friends think it would be wonderful if we could get together.

There's one lady who has decided to make it her business to see if she can get us anywheres together.

[My son] is downright ignorant[7] about it.... And it wouldn't have mattered if it had been Jesus, himself, come back, [he] would not have liked him because nobody's ever going to take his father's place *(Eleanor, late fifties)*.

The inhibiting effects of adult children may be significant in women's ideas about remarriage although, for the most part, they have not directly alluded to them. Wu, however, notes that the incidence of remarriage among Canadian widows with children is 93 percent lower than for women without children (1995: 729).

Nonetheless, it was the gossip that was most disturbing in this case. Eleanor was concerned enough about it to refrain from attending the same church as her friend because of the conclusions others might form. She also declined membership on civic committees on which her friend already served. She did not talk about his reaction to the gossip and whether or not he limited his activities in a similar manner.

One woman, Sharon, had a male friend with whom she spent a great deal of time, but she was quite clear and even insistent that she had no intention of marrying again. The strength of her insistence on this point made me think that she had trouble convincing others of the nature of the relationship. Sharon was one of the very few women who had succeeded in developing a more-than-superficial relationship with man in a way that was comfortable to them both. Neither of them wanted to remarry, and neither felt threatened by the other. Sharon was the only one of the three women who still wore her wedding ring.

Sharon and her friend talked to each other a great deal about their late spouses. They went for walks, out to dinner, and took trips together. Sharon believed that they were meant for each other at this point in their lives, and, in fact, thought that this man was part of her husband's taking care of her from the next world. Both needed someone other than their families to talk to about their loss and had succeeded in building reciprocity into their relationship. Sharon read me a note that her friend had written in which he said that he did not know how he would have survived his wife's death without her friendship and sympathetic ear.

Sharon commented that her sons were very supportive of the friendship, "*100 percent,*" while her friend's daughters were more cautious, perhaps believing that this type of cross-gender friendship is impossible to maintain without going to the next step of becoming a couple. Others, who were not members of her family, were also more skeptical about the nature of the liaison. Some thought she was going out too soon.[8] Sharon opined that she and her friend might eventually go their separate ways, but they were the right people at the right time for each other, and both understood and agreed that marriage was not in their future.

Widowers' Attitudes

Some preliminary comparisons with men's attitudes can be provided from a current ongoing study. Recruitment of widowers provides special challenges both because they are few in number and men are generally less likely than women to volunteer as research participants. Twenty-one widowers have been interviewed to date. They have responded to a variety of announcements through newspapers, radio, Meals on Wheels, and the Third Age Centre at St Thomas University. A few men, approached through acquaintances, have also agreed to participate.

Many of these research volunteers have remarried and several others have particular women friends. It is unclear why widowers who had remarried agreed to volunteer while remarried widows did not. This may reflect the differing strength of the identity of widow and widower. "Widow" seems to be a more central aspect of identity (van den Hoonaard, 1997; 2001), one that is strongly associated with being alone. "Widower" seems to be a much less central identity. The term does not conjure up a definite image for men and may imply having lost a wife rather than being currently single. Whatever the explanation, the differences in the samples may contribute to the very different types of findings that begin to emerge when I compare the experiences of men with the women.

The first and most obvious difference between men's and women's thoughts on repartnering is the centrality to men's experience of finding another woman. As mentioned earlier, issues around relationships with women surfaced very early in the interview with men. In fact, two men brought up the issue of repartnering before the interview even began. For example, as I was setting up the tape recorder, I commented that there are many more widows around than widowers. This man responded by saying: *"Well, I know. I can't say that I've been run off my feet with offers or anything. ... But I didn't go out of my way to try it"* (Robert, seventy-two).

Note this man's assumption that the existence of women and the issue of the possibility of repartnering are almost synonymous.

Getting involved with a woman seems to be a much more intrinsic aspect of being a widower than of being a widow—whether the men want to remarry or not, widowers seem to think that repartnering is natural and an indication of not wallowing in grief. One man feels that he is struggling to accept that his wife is gone forever. His acceptance would allow him to develop a relationship with another woman: *"When I meet a very interesting woman, for example, I say, there's a good choice ... and then the powerful load of feelings for my wife is still there ... but I have to spread my feelings to somebody else, and I don't know how to do that. I can't"* (Armand, fifty-nine).

Another contrast between men's and women's attitudes about remarriage concerns men's worry about getting trapped or losing control in a relationship. Women worry about misinterpreting men's actions; men also worry about giving women the wrong impression about their interest: *"The slightest show of interest, and they feel like they might be sending the wrong messages"* (William, sixty).

Getting trapped might also result from a woman's putting pressure on a man for more commitment than he wants to make: *"You invited one person [to a dance], and they said they just liked a companion. ... Well, after a while, she wanted more than that, and I wasn't interested ... and she was quite annoyed"*.

One man felt so much pressure from one woman that he got Caller ID on his phone in order to avoid answering when she called.

Related to the concern of loss of control is some widowers' insistence that they make their own choice about with whom to go out and with whom to get involved. They raised this issue in the context of matchmaking: *"[My family] did not want me to be a lonely, old widower. They actually arranged people. ... But there was no way I was going to, to allow my family to dictate who I was going to be relating to in any way, at any level"* (Michael, eighty-three).

One man even experienced anticipatory matchmaking while his wife, who had been ill for years prior to her death, was still alive.

Another factor that makes some widowers nervous about women is their perception of being chased by widows, sometimes literally. One widower referred to this as "the Casserole Brigade." Some widows concur with this observation. For example, a widow who participated in a study of life in Florida retirement communities remarked that if you bring a casserole during Shiva it is too early, but that if you waited until after Shiva, it is too late (van den Hoonaard, 1994).[9]

However, it is not clear whether or not widowers are always interpreting the women's actions correctly. The simple extending of friendship that Marion described may be misinterpreted as interest in a romantic relationship.

Implicit in many men's comments is their preference for making their own decisions and for being free. Statements contrasting marriage with being free were not uncommon. For example, one man saw being single again as allowing him to date a number of women: "*I felt almost an obsession to get involved [with a woman]. I'm **free now**; I can do anything I damn please*" (Michael, eighty-three) [emphasis added].

In contrast, when women talked about freedom in widowhood, they spoke of things like being able to vacuum in the middle of the night if they could not sleep and not having to be home at a particular time in order to cook supper.

Nonetheless, interviews with widowers suggest that men are, indeed, more interested in remarriage than women, almost half having a significant relationship with a woman. Some of the men have said that they "*cannot live alone*," and one described the phenomenon as "*the empty-house syndrome*." Women, in contrast, seem pleasantly surprised at how well they do living alone. Doyle et al. (1994) have shown that older Canadian women not only manage living alone but also come to enjoy and value it.

One man has told me that he began to go out on dates "*just to keep busy*" (Samuel, eighty-three). He described his life without his wife as "*meaningless*" and told me about a "*weekend girlfriend*" he had had for a time. He had a serious girlfriend at the time of our interview and has since married. The salience of a connection to another woman also fills the void created by a wife's not being there to make the social contacts, remember birthdays, and keep up with family commitments.

Conclusion

It is clear from the material in this article that widows have to reconstruct completely the ways they deal with men after their husbands die. They need to be careful that they both do not send the wrong message, that is, that they are interested in pursuing a romantic and/or intimate relationships with a man, and that they interpret the actions and words of men correctly. One way to handle this is to continue to wear a wedding ring and to avoid one-on-one social contact with men. Even if the women are interested in marriage, they are faced with changed sexual conventions, suspicious children, gossip, and men who think that everyone is after them.

Women who do not have a couple relationship with a man tend to live in a social world comprised primarily of women. They are comfortable traveling with another woman or going out to restaurants with a group of women. Men, on the other hand, do not find such companionship among other men and, therefore, often report a daughter or other female relative who is both confidante and traveling or social-event companion. Moore and Stratton (2002: 196) found that widowers they spoke to in the United States almost always had what they call a "current woman," a woman who is not a romantic or intimate partner but is available as a "date" or traveling companion. Canadian widowers seem to conform to this pattern.

There are obvious and significant differences between men's and women's overall experience and understanding about being widowed not the least of which are their attitudes and experiences with the opposite sex. In some ways these differences are paradoxical. Women are less interested in repartnering but do not feel very threatened by the possibility of getting more involved than they want. In contrast, men are more interested in remarriage or repartnering but appear to be more worried about getting trapped into a relationship that is more serious than they want and that would impinge upon their freedom.

Notes

1. This study is funded by a grant from the Social Sciences and Humanities Research Council of Canada.
2. Unless otherwise stated, all quotations are taken verbatim from the interviews. All names are pseudonyms.
3. This symbol of removing the ring as an indication of willingness to remarry is not unique to New Brunswick. In an earlier study of a condominium-type retirement community in Florida, a widow remarked that taking off one's ring signifies an interest in remarriage (van den Hoonaard, 1994).
4. June made observations several times during the interview about aspects of widowhood that she had had to face gradually during her husband's decline (Rosenthal and Dawson, 1991).
5. In my current study of widowers, however, there are two men who are not married but living with women.
6. Audrey has now married although I do not know if it is to the same person she was seeing at the time of our interview.
7. In New Brunswick parlance, "ignorant" does not mean unaware; rather it means

rude or overbearing.
8. Widows often face the judgment of others if they seem to be recovering from their grief too quickly, perhaps because others feel they are not being loyal to their husbands. For example, one woman in Florida told me that she had been criticized for going swimming too soon after her husband died.
9. This woman in lived a retirement community that was predominately Jewish. Shiva is the official period of mourning, usually one week or one month.

References

Adams, R. G. (1985). People would talk: Normative barriers to cross-sex friendship for elderly women. *The Gerontologist*, 25(6): 605-611.

Caine, L. (1974). *Widow*. New York: William Morrow.

Davidson, K. (1999). Gender, age and widowhood: How older widows and widowers differently realign their lives. Ph.D. Thesis, University of Surrey, Guildford, UK.

Doyle, V., with Backman, B., Cassiday, E., Cumby, B., Ferneyhouch, B., Floreczyk, J., Gladman, W., Hall, P., Joyce, P., MacLean, A., Miller, M., Rafferty, P., Riley, R., Ritchie, D., Smith, J., Trohan D., and Ward, V. (1994). *It's my turn now: The choice of older women to live alone*. Gerontology Research Centre, Simon Fraser University at Harbour Centre.

Elliot, G., Hunt, M., and Hutchison, K. (1996). *Facts on aging in Canada*. Compiled by the Office of Gerontological Studies, McMaster University, Hamilton, ON.

Hochschild, A. R. (1989). *The second shift: Working parents and the revolution at home*. New York: Viking.

Lopata, H. Z. (1996). *Current widowhood: Myths and realities*. Thousand Oaks, CA: Sage.

Lopata, H. Z. (1981). Widowhood and husband sanctification. *Journal of Marriage and the Family*, 43: 439-50.

Moore, A. J., and Stratton, D. C. (2002). *Resilient widowers: Older men speak for themselves*. New York: Springer.

Rosenthal, C. J., and Dawson, P. (1991). Wives of institutionalized elderly men: The first stage of the transition to quasi-widowhood. *Journal of Aging and Health*, 3(3): 315-334.

Statistics Canada (2001). CANSIM II, Table 051-0010, http://www.statcan.ca/english/Pgdb/People/Families/famil101a.htm.

van den Hoonaard, D. K. (1994). Paradise lost: Widowhood in a Florida retirement community. *Journal of Aging Studies* 8 (2): 121-132.

van den Hoonaard, D. K. (1997). Identity foreclosure: Women's experiences of widowhood as expressed in autobiographical accounts. *Ageing and Society* 17: 533-51.

van den Hoonaard, D. K. (2001). *The widowed self: The older woman's journey through widowhood*. Waterloo, ON: Wilfrid Laurier University Press.

Wright, P. H. (1991). Gender differences in adults' same- and cross-gender friendships. In R. G. Adams and R. Blieszner (Eds.), *Older adult friendship: Structure and process* (pp 197-221). Newbury Park, CA: Sage.

Wu, Z. (1995). Remarriage after widowhood: A marital study of older Canadians. *Canadian Journal on Aging* 14(4): 719-736.

7

The "Current Woman" in an Older Widower's Life

Alinde J. Moore and Dorothy C. Stratton

Gender factors affect a person's life from birth to death, so it could be presumed that the widowhood experience of each gender would be different. Yet, until recently, the scholarly literature on widowhood was almost exclusively about women. When widowed men were studied or when they were compared with widowed women, the focus was narrow. No one had asked widowers the broad question: What is the experience of widowhood for older men? This became the basic research question for our qualitative study of fifty-one widowed men ranging in age from fifty-eight to one hundred and four years. Interviews were conducted from January of 1997 through April of 2000. The men lived in eleven states scattered throughout the United States and in two Canadian provinces; their origins were even more diverse. Many of the men whom we found in retirement areas had come from many different states. Two were born in Europe, one in Asia. As ours was a study of adjustment to widowhood, most of the participants had been widowed at least two years.

The study yielded many interesting findings that illuminated the lives and the concerns of this group of men. One of the most intriguing findings was that almost every man in the study had at the time of the interview a significant *sustaining* relationship with a certain

---

Portions of this chapter are drawn from the book, *Resilient Widowers: Older Men Speak for Themselves*, and appear here with permission granted by Springer Publishing Company, New York.

woman on whom he could rely (Moore and Stratton, 2001). We term this common occurrence the *current woman* in the widowed man's life. A current woman is one who takes over at least some part of a deceased wife's role, or does something beneficial for the man that his wife had stopped doing, or perhaps had never done. The relationship is some enduring combination of practical help, friendship, and companionship. Many relationships include intimacy which may or may not include sexual behavior.

Literature Review

There are many more older women than older men. The U. S. Bureau of the Census (1993) counted approximately nineteen million women and thirteen million men over the age of sixty-five years. With increasing age, the ratio of women to men increases. The U. S. Census records only the current marital status of respondents, thereby not recording the widowhood experience of people who have remarried. Given the sex ratio in the older age groups, older widowed men have a large pool of potential new mates and so are more able than women to remarry, if they wish to do so. They are less likely than women to appear in the census as widowed because they are more likely to have remarried. Therefore reflecting only current status and not the totality of widowhood experiences, the Bureau of the Census (1993) counted 10.2 per cent of men aged sixty-five to seventy-four as widowed, and 23.7 per cent of men age seventy-five and older.

Thompson's *Older Men's Lives* (1994) opens with a discussion of older men's invisibility. Older women have been studied more than older men because they are more numerous, but also because they are a disadvantaged population, generally having fewer resources than men, and are therefore of more interest to social scientists. Society tends to homogenize its conception of elderly people, Thompson writes, and that common image is female.

The literature on gender differences in coping with widowhood, remarriage, and friendship contribute to an understanding of the "current woman" phenomenon. While being able to remarry quickly may seem to be an advantage for men, there is correspondingly no *society of widowers* (as there is a society of widows) for the widowed men who do not remarry (Vinick, 1978:360). Berardo (1970) considered aged widowers on their own and painted a dismal picture of their isolation and failure to adapt. Vinick found widowed men to be more limited than widowed women in relationships with family and friends, less experienced with household management, and having retired, no longer regularly visiting familiar locales in which they might meet other people. In our study, we found that over half of the unmarried, widowed participants relieved loneliness with a dating relationship or a non-romantic relationship with a woman.

Ferraro et al. (1984) propose a compensation model, wherein people who have faced a stressful loss find alternative means of meeting needs and gaining social support. The ability to relate as a friend or to form new friendships may be low during acute grieving, but after three or four years, the person may have more friends than before, having compensated for the loss of companionship by reaching out to others. In widowhood, elderly people receive the most social and emotional support from family, with friends ranking next. Crohan and Antonucci (1989) report that both family and friends impact positively an older person's well-being and life satisfaction.

Johnson and Troll (1994) found that nearly half of people over age eighty-five said they were still making new friends. Johnson and Troll found that older people expand friendship possibilities by redefining who is a friend to include acquaintances and by accepting the idea of friendship as existing without the opportunity for face-to-face interaction. While Wright (1982) concludes that there are many more similarities than differences in the friendship patterns of older men and women, others claim that male friendships are based on shared activities while female friendships are based on intimacy (Seidler, 1992).

Allan (1989) and Swain (1992) note that it is easier for men to talk to women about relationships and personal lives – an expression of intimacy that would be missed with the death of a wife. Lowenthal and Haven (1968) argue that men typically have no confidante other than wife. Similarly, Preston and Grimes (1987) find that married men rely heavily on their spouses for emotional support. Stevens (1995) reports that widowers rely on their children or new partners, while widows develop a broader support network including neighbors and friends. Hagestad (1986) found that second wives kept the men connected with their families in ways that they apparently could not do well on their own.

Being paired with a woman may seem to be "doing what comes naturally"; it may represent a special attraction and affinity between genders, a combination of comfort, complementarity, and the familiar tension of natural and socialized differences. A widowed man may be seeking someone to fulfill long-accustomed roles of daily-task performance, an emotional foil for one who learned not to express his emotions fully, someone with whom to go out in a decidedly couples' society, someone who likes to go to places and do things that men are not supposed to like to do on their own, such as dining in nice restaurants, going to the theater, or going on a cruise. A woman may be someone to talk to in an accustomed way.

Methodology

Our methodology was guided by the *grounded theory* approach of Glaser and Strauss (1967). Early findings contributed new understandings and helped to ground subsequent interviews in the lives of these older men. We conducted the interviews ourselves using an ethnographic interviewing style (Spradley, 1979) to elicit topics, information, and feeling content from the men. Nearly all of the interviews were conducted in the men's homes so we could observe their surroundings. All but three of the participants were citizens of the United States; one was from India, two were Canadian. All were living in the United States, except one Canadian (one Canadian "snowbird" divided his time between Canada and the USA—we interviewed him in Florida). The men were recruited using personal and professional contacts. We sought men who were at least sixty years of age and who had been widowed at least two years. We strove for diversity in race and ethnicity, geographic location, socioeconomic class, religion, and educational level. Because we could interview only in English, our sample is lacking widowed men who spoke only another language. Because we did not use random sampling techniques, we do not claim that our findings are representative of older widowed men in general. However, our diverse sample of fifty-one men yielded a wealth of data which has illuminated for us older men's circumstances and the patterns of their lives. The transcribed interviews were coded and analyzed using QSR NUD*IST software.

Findings

Nearly all of the men in our study had a significant sustaining relationship with a woman at the time of our interview. Not all of the relationships included intimacy in the sense of sexual closeness, but most included warm and caring personal relations that meet a broader definition of intimacy. Loneliness was a feeling that our respondents freely acknowledged. We found most of the men interested in companionship, but they expressed divergent views regarding remarriage.

For some men the current woman was another wife. For many others it was an adult daughter. Some men had relied on an adult daughter during the immediate bereavement phase but later found a new wife or a "companion." Female companions were the current woman for several men, ranging from committed live-in relationships to women neighbors or church members with whom the men regularly engaged in some type of social activity (typically, eating out or watching videos at one home or the other). Participants described companionship arrangements that ran the spectrum of intimacy. Most that were sexual also included a significant component of emotional closeness. Some involved steady dating, but with an understanding that sex was not part of the relationship. A few companionship arrangements seemed to be somewhat conflicted in tone, but were convenient in terms of "having someone to do something with."

Once having identified these more common categories of current woman, we found that some men, by reason of necessity, convenience or creative social maneuvering, had fashioned another type of relationship. Some had reestablished a close relationship with a sister or had developed close ties with a granddaughter or niece. It was interesting to note situations of closeness with daughters-in-law. While most sons seemed quite interested in the welfare of their widowed fathers, the utilitarian relationship and usually some emotional closeness developed with the daughter-in-law. Ned's daughter-in-law fondly called him "Dad." Bapuji lived with his son and daughter-in-law; it was she who spent mornings with him before going to work. Bruce described his daughter-in-law as a confidante and the person who would probably take care of him if he needed help.

Childless widowers demonstrated social adeptness at establishing a relationship with a woman. Friendliness with a neighbor, a work colleague, or a service provider sometimes led to a supportive personal relationship. Neighbors, church members, and work colleagues were frequently supportive even in cases where the widowed men had children, as they were close at hand when the children may have been living elsewhere.

Even the most introverted men had a current woman relationship. In fact, the more introverted men seemed to find that one person to be close to more quickly than others, perhaps in that way eliminating the need to interact with many people or to undertake a prolonged search for companionship. One such man said he was not sure how he met and courted his current wife; it just happened, and he found himself married five months after his first wife had died.

Only a few of the men we interviewed had no one woman who could be identified as sustaining in their current life. These men, for the main part fairly independent people, interacted with both men and women, obviously seeing that their socializing needs were met, but not depending upon any one person on a regular basis. Two men were loners, having only brief and superficial contact with anyone.

Relationship Patterns

The relationships described by the participants can be placed in six categories: (a) interaction based on practical help, (b) activity-based friendship, (c) filial-type companionship, (d) partner relationship without sexual activity, (e) partner relationship including sexual activity, (f) remarriage.

The categories range from the cordiality of a helpful neighbor to the intimacy of a new marriage. In general, categories (a) and (b) do not involve the warmth and closeness that is integral to the other categories. Our participants frequently used the term *companion* to refer to the sustaining woman in their life. We chose the term *partner* to indicate relationships in which the two people would be viewed as a couple.

The distribution of participants in our study is shown in table 7.1.

Current woman relationships are much more often intimate than not. When the partner relationship categories are added together (for a total of twelve), there is a fairly even distribution of close relationships (thirteen for filial, twelve for partner, fourteen for new wife). It is important to note there is variation in the intensity of involvement within each relationship type. As always, human situations are not neatly categorized. But broad classification helps us to see patterns, such as the importance of family (filial companionship) for the men who are older, disabled and/or frail. Mehta (chapter 8) refers to this phenomenon in a study of late-life Singaporean widows and widowers as the *immediate family cocoon*. She found it served to insu-

Table 7.1

Distribution of Types of Relationship

(a) interaction based on practical help	3
(b) activity-based friendship	5
(c) filial-type companionship	13
(d) partner relationship without sexual activity	4
(e) partner relationship including sexual activity	8
(f) remarriage	14
(g) no current woman	4
Total	51

late or preclude her subjects from the expression of sexual needs in the realm of dating and remarriage. Although many of the widowers in our study had filial-type companionship, we are excluding them from further discussion here as it is not the focus of this book. As we give examples, we refer to many of the participants by their study names.

Interaction Based on Practical Help

A woman could often be counted on to give practical advice about cooking, shopping, and cleaning. For example, one man said his neighbor was happy to tell him how to launder the "ring around the collar" out of his dress shirts. Contacts of this nature may be no more than simple, helpful friendliness. Most women are socialized to be caring, nurturing, and helpful. When a woman sees an opportunity, it may appeal to her to offer help, and it may please her when she sees that she has helped someone. She may derive extra satisfaction from helping a man, because of her earlier gender training (women take care of men, women make a home). Conversely, men are socialized "to avoid all things, actions, and reactions that are potentially feminine" (Levant and Pollock, 1998:1-2). In a comparison of older widows and widowers, van den Hoonaard (1994) found the widows much better at taking care of themselves. Similarly, Lund et al. (1993:246) found older men "to be deficient in a predictable set of skills, including cooking, shopping and housecleaning". Those who had learned new skills during bereavement reported feeling better about themselves, more independent, and better able to get along with others; being competent around the house also helped them deal with their grief. Gass (1989) advises those who would help widowers to encourage the development of new roles and skills.

Activity-Based Friendship

Seidler (1992) characterizes men's friendships as based on shared activities, but finding older men with whom to do things is difficult for older widowers. For example, in the age group of eighty-five plus, women outnumber men by two to one, and half of the men are living with and spending their time with spouses (U.S. Bureau of the Census 1999). The numbers available for men's friendships are low to begin with; then disability and death take their toll. The older man who loses a friend will not find him easy to replace. Al for instances loved to play pool and was looking for an opponent, but there were only three other men in his apartment building, and all were disabled. He laughed off the suggestion by the interviewer that he play pool with a woman, but then he mentioned that he enjoyed visiting with the widow in the adjacent apartment.

Playing cards, giving transportation, and dining together are other examples in this category of interaction. Andrew received a phone call during our interview from a lady in his synagogue congregation who was checking on the time he would pick her up for their singing group practice. Claude commented that the lady next door tapped on his door as she walked toward the senior apartments' dining room, and then he would join her for the rest of the distance. Richard's neighbor was about thirty years younger and divorced. She would come to his condo every morning and fix breakfast for the two of them and eat with him. She also took him on outings, such as to lunch with her mother who lived in a nursing home. Will had a much younger companion with whom he frequently went to dinner and to cultural events; they offered each other support and intellectual stimulation. The townfolks in their small town speculated on the nature of the relationship. According to Swain (1992), cross-sex friendships are often interpreted as romances or sexual relationships, and claims of "just being friends" are regarded as withholding information about the sexual or romantic nature of the relationship. In all of these examples, the relationships were stable and appreciated by both parties, but they had less of a sense of intimacy than the others.

Partner Relationship Without Sexual Activity

Bulcroft and Bulcroft (1991), using the National Survey of Families, found their subjects aged sixty years and older dating for the purpose of companionship and with the hopes of developing a stable, companionate relationship. The majority of the men we interviewed were indeed seeking a new partner relationship and our findings show that men who do this are likely to succeed. However, we found some men preferred a non-sexual steady relationship. The reasons they gave include: (a) not believing in sex without marriage; (b) not feeling sexual attraction, usually related to feelings towards deceased wife; (c) being impotent; or (d) feeling too old to get involved.

John for instance had a woman friend from church, and then another. He liked the companionship, but he was very wary of anything that might lead to the possibility of marriage. Arch's enduring relationship with his older neighbor was hard to define; they traveled together, they apparently aggravated each other over differences on various issues and apparently were not sexually involved. The relationship was steady and certainly provided companionship. Kenneth liked going out to eat with his partner, but said he avoided sexual involvement because of impotence.

Partner Relationship Including Sexual Activity

Study participants tended to have strong opinions regarding the types of intimate relationships they thought appropriate. The variety in these opinions reflects the trend in society away from the importance of a legally sanctioned marriage. However, as in society as a whole, there were many who still felt that being married was the only acceptable circumstance for a sexual relationship. Stuart, for example, said he and his second wife did not sleep together until they were married. That to him signified the respect that they both had for the new relationship. He acknowledged that they had given up quite a lot financially to enter the new marriage, but that nothing mattered more than doing the whole thing right. Vinick (1983) found more than seventy-five percent of unmarried widower participants disapproving of living together without remarriage. Most of the men in our study had internalized the propriety of being married to one's sexual intimate. Those who held most strongly to it at the time of the interview did so for religion-based reasons, although they spoke more of "rightness" than of the need to follow the rules of their denomination. For them there was not a decision to be made about whether to marry the woman with whom they wanted an intimate relationship; that was simply the way it would be done.

A few of the men seemed to have no discomfort in admitting their acceptance of a non-marital sexual relationship. These men either did not have a religious base for their decision-making, or felt that the rules of their denomination did not affect their choices.

Some study participants considered the change in social mores and then came to their own conclusions. Usually, they were persuaded by dollars and cents that a new legal marriage was too costly. Frank's partner would have had to give up her deceased husband's military pension. Clyde's partner would have lost more than $500 a month from her deceased husband's black lung benefits. *"She was wanting to marry me,"* he said, *"but I told her I didn't think I was worth that much to her. What if I would die in the next year, or the next few days? Then she wouldn't have nothing."* "How accepting was she of that statement?" the interviewer inquired. Clyde laughed, *"Yeah, she seconded it and said a man wasn't worth $500 a month to her."*

In most of these situations, the practical consideration of finances prevailed, although the presumed opinions of others, especially their own adult children, could sway the men in the direction of marriage. Bulcroft and Bulcroft (1991) claimed that ninety percent of the daters aged sixty years and older in their sample were having a sexual relationship. In the relationships we identified as partners, the sexual relationships were twice as numerous as the non-sexual (i. e., eight and four). We presume some men presented their current woman relationships as nonsexual when they were not, because the men might not have felt comfortable sharing the situation with an interviewer whom they might have perceived as daughterly. Others who did not have a partner relationship at the time seemed clear about how they would feel if given the opportunity to experience one. Jerry said that he and his wife had been virgins when they married, but now, more than thirty years later, he spoke of the possibility of living with a woman without marriage by saying, *"If I met someone now, and that would happen, I would do it in a minute."*

Enjoying the independence of living alone while having the companionship of a pleasant person when that was mutually agreeable was an ideal situation for the partnered men and their companions. Such arrangements are described as Living Apart Together (LAT) (for instance de Jong Gierveld [chapter 5]; Ghazanfareeon Karlsson and Borell [chapter 1]; Levine and Trost, 1999). Rubinstein (1986) describes the intimate companion as a same-cohort confidante with whom the widowed man has a special bond, without giving up his independent lifestyle and the haven of his home. Charles and his partner ate together in the retirement community dining hall and watched TV together, but they joked about not inviting each other over to eat at their own apartments because they did not want to get an obligatory pattern started. Extended visits to a partner in another state worked well for Clyde; he could maintain his own home space, which he did not want changed in any way. Joe and his long-time partner went dancing together and would *"play house when we want to."*

The situation was not always mutually agreeable. As mentioned earlier, Kenneth enjoyed going out to dinner regularly, but his companion was more interested in marriage than he. George and his long-time companion had agreed not to marry when they began their dating; he later proposed to her, but she said she wanted to keep their independent arrangements. He agreed to that.

The men who remarried tended to marry someone close to them in age. Conversely, we found that the relationships that involved greater age differences tended not to result in marriage. When the woman was older by more than just a few years, the couple did not marry, even though in three out of the four situations where the widowed man was younger than his companion, the relationship included sex. One man, who lived by values expressing great tolerance, said nevertheless that his partner's older age was of concern to him in thinking about marriage. The stereotype growing out of the social custom of men marrying younger women seemed to affect men's thinking about marrying an older woman. Conversely, when the widowed man was much older than his partner, neither marriage nor a sexual relationship was likely. Berardo et al. (1993) found that age disparities in marriage increase with ages of the people marrying and are greater in remarriages, but also found that extreme age disparities are rare in any case. Their findings are in keeping with ours; match-ups close in age were much more likely to marry than companionable arrangements where parties were far apart in age.

The Importance of Sex

This topic was not particularly comfortable for the men to discuss with a younger female interviewer, although the question was posed late in the interviewing process when rapport had been firmly established. Also, the question was asked obliquely: *"Would you comment on the importance of a sexual relationship to an older man?"* One very old man responded gently, *"I wouldn't have anything to say about that. "* A few others responded, *"Yes, it is important,"* and changed the subject. One expressed his embarrassment with a somewhat lengthy and oblique analogy about various types of waning appetites. One remarried man blurted out a joking little story about *"bouncing the springs."* Bill, also remarried, was an exception within our study. He initiated a discussion of sex, spoke very favorably of nudity, and displayed a *Playboy* magazine on the coffee table where the interview took place.

Typically, however, the response was brief and affirmed that a sexual relationship was viewed positively. One man said, *"Things speed up and things slow down, and this sort of thing, you hope for and generally you end up with a mutually acceptable situation."* The men also usually conveyed the idea that companionship and the absence of loneliness were the main benefits of a new relationship; sex was nice but not the most important factor. A man in his eighties said that, *"Neither the man nor the woman is still capable,"* but that other things such as companionship and sharing similar interests are more important. A younger remarried participant said, *"At this point in my life, that sexual relationship is a pleasant and good bonding experience. There's no urgency about it. It's something that we both enjoy."* One man said of course he did not remarry for sex; he could buy that!

For men of advanced age and experiencing health decline, remarriage or any sexual relationship did not seem to be a practical possibility. Several had prostate difficulties, including cancer. Others had heart disease or significant mobility problems. Their comments during the interview were some version of "not interested" or "cannot do." Erikson et al. (1986) refer to "unchosen celibacy." That was the case for the men in our study who were not in a sexual relationship. Some of the older men probably said they had no interest in sex anymore because their bodies and health had failed them in that regard. Some of the men were still bonded to the memory of their deceased wife and would not think of having another relationship. They accepted and kept the unchosen celibacy. Others who had had a very good marriage appreciated the marriage situation so much that they sought another woman for an intimate relationship (including but not limited to sex).

Talbott's (1998) findings regarding the attitudes of older widows towards men and remarriage mirror our findings of older widowers' attitudes toward remarriage. Widowed people of both genders are less likely to remarry if they saw their first marriage as very poor, if they saw their first marriage as too wonderful to be replaced, if they were in poor health, or if they were older than average when widowed. It should be noted that in this study of men who had been in long-term heterosexual marriages, we found no participant who expressed or conveyed any sexual interest in other men.

Remarriage

Older men have a statistical advantage when it comes to remarriage. As mentioned before, the thirteen million men over age sixty-five in 1992 had approximately nineteen million potential female partners over age sixty-five (U. S. Bureau of the Census 1993). Kuhn et al. (1993) reported the overall marriage rate for older men was six times higher than the marriage rate for older women, reflecting both the higher numbers of women and the tendency for men to marry younger women.

The components of marital intimacy can be described as (a) physical and emotional closeness; (b) intellectual compatibility—being able to talk about things that matter; and (c) the supportive and practical helpmate role. There is much to miss when a marriage is lost. Some of the men who described their first marriages as very good were eager to remarry so they could experience all those good aspects of marriage in their lives again. But even if the first marriage had not been very positive, the comfort of a routine that included another person made remarriage attractive.

What did men gain from remarriage? They gained companionship, sexual intimacy, caregiving, activity-based friendship, and someone to do the chores and serve as social secretary. We found second wives who were superlative "kin-keepers" (Hagestad, 1986). They knew more about their new husband's children than the husbands did. For example, Garrett's second wife had been a good friend of his first wife. He called out to her in a far room of the house several times when the interviewer asked about his children and their families. Finally we agreed that she would join us in the last minutes of the interview to provide this information.

There is a stereotype of widowed men remarrying quickly. We found that a few of the men in our study did remarry quickly, but only fourteen of the fifty-one men had remarried overall. Given that women are far more numerous than men in the older age groups, men can generally remarry if they want to. Women may not have the choice, or as Davidson (chapter 4) points out, may not choose to remarry. Burch (1990) comments on the low remarriage rate for Canadian widowers noting that many may be making the choice not to remarry. However, researchers have noted the benefits of remarriage for men (Burks et al., 1988; Davidson, 2001; Gupta, 1999). Gentry and Shulman (1988:192) state, "Widowers may remarry more frequently than widows because they are more dependent on marriage for their well-being." van den Hoonaard (1994) studied widowed people in a Florida retirement community. She noted men were more eager to remarry because they experienced more difficulty in living alone.

The men in our study varied in length of widowhood, so we expected there would be changes in interest toward remarriage as the time spent in widowhood lengthened. Actually, we found stability in the men's positions on remarriage. Our population had been selected from men who (except for three) had been widowed at least two years. Our findings show that many widowed men "hook up" rapidly with a woman companion, whether or not marriage was the outcome. Thus, the forty-eight participants who were two years or more past their loss were in an adjustment stage for the most part beyond acute grieving and had spent time thinking about their futures and getting a sense of their feelings. However, even the three men who were more recently widowed at the time of the interview were able to make clear a position on remarriage that had not changed when we followed up with them the next year.

Only three of the forty unmarried men remarried after the interview, also demonstrating continuity. One was about to remarry at the time of the interview. Another was very anxiously seeking a new spouse, whom he found in about a year. The last expressed interest in dating at the time of the interview and married a little more than a year later.

Only a few of the men demonstrated a shift in interest regarding remarriage. Daniel became interested in another marriage when he met a particularly compatible woman. John became interested in companionship and perhaps remarriage after his acute grieving, but he shifted away from that interest as he worried about various negative possibilities. The result was a more cautious man who would probably continue to find reasons not to remarry.

Finding a New Spouse

Lopata's (1979) research showed that widowed women tended to marry someone they already knew. It was the same for the men in our study. The women whom the men married fell into distinct categories, with the most common being a widowed woman whom they knew before they were widowed. The categories are as follows:

Someone already known. Sam married his deceased wife's widowed sister, Sy and Malcolm each married a widowed neighbor, Garrett his wife's best friend who was a widow, Benjamin a very distant widowed relative whom he met at a reunion, Russell an old sweetheart widowed after a marriage to someone else, Bill a long-widowed cousin of his first wife. Henrik married the nurse who took care of his wife during her long illness; she had been widowed twice.

Someone met on his own after wife died. Walter met his new wife at his new retirement community, Terrence and Kenneth at work, Daniel at synagogue, Alvin through social activities. All of these new wives had been widowed.

Someone met through connections. Stuart's sister referred him to a widowed woman with whom she worked.

Someone met through advertising. Earl placed an ad in the local newspaper and from many responses eventually married a divorced woman.

Discussion

Negotiation

Negotiation between a widowed man and a current woman involved coming to an understanding on the nature of the relationship, and the degree of closeness that was comfortable (allowable) now and potentially in the future, especially regarding sexual activity, exclusivity, and commitment. The benefits of a new relationship must be weighed by each partner against the loss of independence as de Jong Gierveld discusses in chapter 5. Motivation and perception of motivation become part of the negotiation process. A woman may offer a man help with no other expectation, or she may be seeking a closer relationship when she offers help. Either party may perceive the other's interest as being something other than just a simple act of giving and receiving help. If neither person has a partner at the time, they each will be reading the signals of the other. Men's friendships with women that do not have sexual activity, overtones or potential are not very common (see also chapter 6 by van den Hoonaard). Swain refers to "ambiguous sexual boundaries," stating that both "women and men questioned the reality of the 'platonic' friendship" (1992:164), feeling the sexual dynamic of the relationship could change. Alvin told the interviewer of his friendships with several women, but Alvin clearly wanted another wife, and the women with whom he interacted would certainly have been aware of that. Men who simply wanted companionship for dinner in a restaurant sometimes were reluctant to ask a woman out, for fear of creating expectations. George pointed out that women developed those expectations far too easily. He said he would take someone out, but then he would get phone calls asking, *"Well, how come you didn't call me?"* He was too polite to say so, but he said he thought, *"I only took you out one time, lady. You know what I mean?"* Michael said he would receive calls from women. His policy was to take them out to dinner once, but not again.

Most of the men recalled the customs and expectations from their long-ago courtships and were nervous about the new expectations they might encounter now. Jerry described the senior dating scene as, *"Akin to an hour on the rack"* and *"My worst nightmare."* Stuart asked the interviewer how one could reenter the dating scene after many, many years of being out of it. Not only have expectations changed, but senior dating involves a reality that does not interfere with dating at a young age: the dating relationship brings together two long histories of adult life that must be negotiated to a comfort level as Gierveld discusses. Terrence commented, *"I was offered sex before I even dated them. "* He added, *"I didn't want to have sex with any of these ladies and then see them later* (around town)." Earl found advertising successful; he married a woman who answered his ad. However, Michael's ad for a travel companion yielded a poor arrangement. Hence, it seemed that the men who married someone they already knew were the lucky ones; they had been able to avoid the anxiety-producing seniors' dating scene of the late twentieth century.

The *casserole ladies* are a retirement community urban legend. Supposedly legions of them descend upon the doorstep of every newly widowed man (van den Hoonaard 1994). We asked our widower participants about this phenomenon. One man laughed and said no, they had not come, but he wished they had. Yussef said that old men who thought they were being pursued were *"fantasizing."* However, most participants acknowledged that widowed women had been attentive to them. Richard said he asked them to stop bringing food. He could go out to eat if he wanted to and actually preferred his solitary activities at home.

Two men in a predominantly Jewish retirement community had experienced the phenomenon rather fully. Their responses to it were illuminating on the subject of male initiative. Benjamin said that he received a "very strange letter" from a former neighbor, in which she had enclosed her photo; he said he never responded. He said he had "*some fear of females who are more aggressive than others in that respect,*" but could "*appreciate that when they lost their spouse, they felt that part of their life was gone.*" Sy said that he found several women attentive, one in particular was offering to help him deal with his loneliness, but the woman who caught his attention and became his second wife was a nearby neighbor who did not try to get his attention. "*I took a liking to her,*" he said.

Several men who had not remarried spoke modestly of women, particularly at church, having been attentive and of knowing that they could have remarried if they had wanted to. One man residing in a nursing home commented, "*Yeh, I have two or three here who I could move in with anytime, but I'm not interested.*" Ned found, even as he approached his hundreth birthday, a woman at church regularly lingering around him after the service. It would not be overstating the situation to say that all of the men in our study could have remarried if they had wished to. They could all recall women who would have been willing if they had been willing. The opportunity to remarry is a major difference between widows and widowers created by the imbalance in gender longevity and the social custom of men marrying younger women.

In two of the marriages, the wife had already been widowed twice before. The interviewers met these women and had the opportunity to observe the interaction of the spouses briefly, but the women were not actually interviewed. When an older woman undertakes her third marriage after two widowhood experiences, one might conclude that she feels a strong need or desire to be married. Walter's second wife was very talkative and energetic in contrast to his inexpressiveness. He said he knew he was holding her back from activities with her friends, but she spoke in glowing terms of his positive qualities, his first marriage, and their marriage together. Benjamin's wife was pleasant and energetic; she chided him in front of the interviewer for his slow driving. It seemed that she was the more dominant personality in the relationship. In both cases the wives appeared to be more energetic and active. Walter's wife put a glow on the marriage and everything else in life. Benjamin's wife seemed to tease as a mild way of attempting to change him. Neither marriage was bad; it just appeared upon brief observation that the couples were having to work through some differences in personal style. This could be the result of individuals marrying out of a need to be married, and then working through the adjustments that were needed to sustain the relationship.

Comparing or Not

Grinwald and Shabat (1997:107) describe the ways in which a dead spouse intrudes into a new marriage: (a) there is endless opportunity for comparison with the new spouse through the "prism of the first marriage"; (b) plans not fulfilled in the first marriage may be carried out in the second; and (c) in-law relations still exist with the deceased spouse's family. Moss and Moss (1980) found that sharing about the past was supportive of a new marriage, but that direct comparing was not.

A new wife can fill the void left by the death of previous wife in all-important roles. That is not to say how the quality of the two relationships would compare. Indeed, most of the men seemed not inclined to compare the two women. The wife that they had lost was the one with whom they had made a home and a family, the one with whom they had matured and aged, the one whose loss they had grieved. The new wife was their loving companion now.

Men would indicate their reluctance or refusal to compare by speaking of the pleasures or the realities of the two relationships independently. However, sometimes comparisons would slip into their comments. One man spoke of his current wife's love of traveling and about the similarities in the kinds of trips that they enjoyed. *"My first wife did not like to travel like that,"* he said, *"so we are really having a good time now."* Another man spoke in a kind and understanding way of his first wife, who had lost interest in sex during a long period of declining health. He then sparkled when he exclaimed about how much his new wife enjoyed sex. "[My first wife] *would complain if I woke her up when I was getting into bed, but* [my second wife] *doesn't care when I wake her up. We're having a great time!"* On the other hand, comparisons sometimes ran in the other direction. *"This marriage is good for both of us,"* one man commented, *"but nothing could be like the first time."* Another made a similar comment, but gave indications that his second marriage was not really good. Having a healthy second wife, Stuart said he now realized how much his first wife's health problems had burdened her through the years. Stuart and Earl felt ambivalent about sharing the joys of retirement with a new wife when their plans had been made with the first wife. Stuart said they had scrimped on expenses in order to save for retirement, and he now regretted not having spent more money earlier so his first wife would have had a more enjoyable life.

Conclusions

Almost all of the men in our study had a sustaining relationship with a woman, a phenomenon we have termed the *current woman*. These relationships ranged from the cordiality of an interaction based on practical help to the intimacy and commitment of a new marriage. Woman friends are chosen for activities which men perceive are appropriate to engage in as a couple – eating out, attending a concert, going on a cruise. A close personal relationship that often involves caregiving characterizes the relationships that many men have with female relatives. This type of help becomes more important and more common as a man's health declines.

Older widowed men value companionship and couples' activities; age and health play important roles in whether or not they consider marrying again. Older men who want a new partner tend to seek and enter a new relationship within months of the death of their spouse. Sex is viewed positively but is only part of a good relationship. Older men seem not to appreciate forwardness in women who are interested in dating. All are lonely but some accommodate themselves to loneliness rather than remarrying because of age, health condition, or devotion to deceased wife, or to avoid what they view as very likely problems. Those who decide to marry tend to marry a widow close to them in age and someone they already have known. First wives are not replaced, but the role of wife is filled with another person. Because older men are so greatly outnumbered by women in their cohort and because it is social custom for men to marry younger women, almost all older men who choose to do so are able to form a new companionate relationship.

References

Allan, G. (1989). *Friendship: Developing a sociological perspective*. San Francisco, CA: Westview.

Avioli, P. S. (1989). The social support functions of siblings in later life. *American Behavioral Scientist*, 33: 45-57.

Berardo, F.M., J. Appel and D.H. Berardo (1993). Age dissimilar marriages: Review and assessment. *Journal of Aging Studies*, 7 (1): 93-106.

Berardo, F. M. (1970). Survivorship and social isolation: The case of the aged widower. *The Family Coordinator*, 19 (1): 11-25.

Bulcroft, R. A. and K. A. Bulcroft (1991). The nature and functions of dating in later life. *Research on Aging*, 13(2): 244-260.

Burch, T. K. (1990). Remarriage of older Canadians: Description and interpretation. *Research on Aging*, 12(4): 546-559.

Burks, V. K., D. A. Lund, C. H. Gregg, and H. P. Bluhm (1988). Bereavement and remarriage for older adults. *Death Studies*, 12: 51-60.

Cicirelli, V. G. (1977). Relationship of siblings to the elderly person's feelings and concerns. *Journal of Gerontology*, 32 (3): 317-322.

Cicirelli, V. G. (1982). Sibling influence throughout the life span. In M.E. Lamb and B. Sutton-Smith (eds.), *Sibling relationships: Their nature and significance across the lifespan*, pp. 267-284. Hillsdale, NJ: Erlbaum.

Connidis, I. A. (1989). Siblings as friends in later life. *American Behavioral Scientist*, 33(1), 81-93.

Crohan, S. E. and T. C. Antonucci (1989). Friends as a source of social support in old age. In R.G. Adams and R. Blieszner (eds.) *Older adult friendship: Structure and process*, pp. 129-145. Newbury Park, CA: Sage Publications.

Davidson, K. (2001). Reconstructing life after a death: Psychological adaptation and social role transition in the medium and long term for older widowed men and women in the UK. *Indian Journal of Gerontology*, 15(1-2): 221-236.

Davidson, K. (2002). Gender differences in new partnership choices and constraints for older widows and widowers. *Ageing International* 27(4): 43-60. (Chapter 4 in this volume.)

de Jong Gierveld, J. D. (2002). The dilemma of repartnering: Considerations of older men and women entering new intimate relationships in later life. *Ageing International*, 27(4): 61-78. (Chapter 5 in this volume.)

Erikson, E. H., J. M. Erikson, and H. Q. Kivnick (1986). *Vital involvement in old age*. New York: Norton.

Ferraro, K. F., E. Mutran, and C. M. Barresi (1984). Widowhood, health, and friendship support in later life. *Journal of Health and Social Behavior*, 25: 245-259.

Gass, K. A. (1989). Health of older widowers: role of appraisal, coping, resources, and types of spouses's death. In D. A. Lund (ed.) *Older bereaved spouses: Research with practical applications*, pp. 95-110. New York: Hemisphere Publishing.

Gentry, M. and A. D. Shulman (1988). Remarriage as a coping response for widowhood. *Psychology and Aging*, 3: 191-196.

Ghazanfareeon Karlsson, S. and K. Borell (2002). Intimacy and autonomy, gender and ageing: Living apart together, *Ageing International* 27(4): 11-26. (Chapter 1 in this volume.)

Glaser, B.G. and A.L. Strauss (1967). *The discovery of grounded theory: Strategies for qualitative research*. New York: Aldine de Gruyter.

Gold, D. T. (1989). Sibling relationships in old age: A typology. *International Journal of Aging and Human Development*, 28 (1): 37-51.

Gold, D. T. (1990). Late-life sibling relationships: Does race affect typological distribution? *The Gerontologist,* 30(6), 741-748.
Grinwald, S. and T. Shabat (1997). The invisible figure of the deceased spouse in remarriage. *Journal of Divorce and Remarriage,* 26(3/4): 105-113.
Gupta, S. (1999). The effects of transitions in marital status on men's performance of housework. *Journal of Marriage and the Family,* 61: 700-711.
Hagestad, G. O. (1986). The aging society as a context for family life. *Daedelus,* 115(1): 119-140.
Hoffman, L. W., K. A. McManus and Y. Brackbill (1987). The value of children to young and elderly parents. *International Journal of Aging and Human Development,* 25 (4): 309-322.
Johnson, C. L. and L. E. Troll (1994). Constraints and facilitators to friendships in late late life. *The Gerontologist,* 34 (1): 79-87.
Kuhn, D. R., D. J. Morhardt and G. Monbrod-Framburg (1993). Late-life marriages, older stepfamilies, and Alzheimer's disease. *Families in Society,* 74(3): 154-162.
Langer, N. (1990). Grandparents and adult grandchildren: What do they do for one another? *International Journal of Aging and Human Development,* 31 (2): 101-110.
Levant, R. F. and W. S. Pollock (eds). (1998). *A new psychology of men.* New York: Basic Books.
Levine, I. and J. Trost (1999). Living apart together. *Community, Work and Family,* 2(3): 279-294.
Lopata, H. Z. (1979). *Women as widows: Support systems.* New York: Elsevier.
Lowenthal, M. and C. Haven (1968). Interaction adaptation: Intimacy as a critical variable. *American Sociological Review,* 33: 20-30.
Mehta, K. K. (2002). Perceptions of remarriage by widowed people in Singapore. *Ageing International,* 27(4): 93-107. (Chapter 8 in this volume.)
Moore, A.J. and D.C. Stratton (2001). *Resilient widowers: Older men speak for themselves.* New York: Springer Publishing.
Moss, M. S. and S. Z. Moss (1980). The image of the deceased spouse in remarriage of elderly widow(er)'s. *Journal of Gerontological Social Work,* 3(2): 59-70.
Preston, D. and J. Grimes (1987). A study of differences in social support. *Journal of Gerontological Nursing,* 13 (2): 36-40.
Rubenstein, R.L. (1986). *Singular paths: Old men living alone.* Guildford, NY: Columbia University Press.
Seidler, V. J. (1992). Rejection, vulnerability, and friendship. In P.M. Nardi (ed.) *Men's Friendships.* Newbury Park, CA: Sage Publications.
Spradley, J. P. (1979). *The ethnographic interview.* New York: Holt, Rinehart, and Winston.
Stevens, N. (1995). Gender and adaptation to widowhood in later life. *Ageing and Society,* 15: 37-58
Swain, S. O. (1992). Men's friendships with women: Intimacy, sexual boundaries, and the informant role. In P. M. Nardi (ed.) *Men's friendships*, pp. 153-172. Newbury Park, CA: Sage Publications.
Talbott, M. M. (1998). Older widows' attitudes towards men and remarriage. *Journal of Aging Studies,* 12(4): 429-450.
Thompson, E. H., Jr. (ed.) (1994). *Older men's lives.* Thousand Oaks, CA: Sage Publications.
U.S. Bureau of the Census (1999), March. *The older population in the United States: Population characteristics.* (Publication No. PPL-133). Washington, DC: U.S. Government Printing Office.
U.S. Bureau of the Census (1993). *Statistical abstracts of the United States, 1992.* Washington, DC: Government Printing Office.

van den Hoonaard, D. K. (1994). Paradise lost: Widowhood in a Florida retirement community. *Journal of Aging Studies,* 8(2):121-132.

van den Hoonaard, D. K. (2002). Attitudes of older widows and widowers in New Brunswick, Canada towards new partnerships. *Ageing International,* 27(4): 79-92. (Chapter 6 in this volume)

Vinick, B. H. (1978). Remarriage in old age. *The Family Coordinator,* 27(4): 359-63.

Vinick, B. H. (1983). Three years after bereavement: Life-styles of elderly widowers. *Interdisciplinary Topics in Gerontology,* 17: 50-57.

Wright, P. H. (1982). Men's friendships, women's friendships and the alleged inferiority of the latter. *Sex Roles,* 8(1): 1-20.

8

Perceptions of Remarriage by Widowed People in Singapore

Kalyani K. Mehta

Remarriage occurs after one of two types of critical events, divorce or death of spouse. Ganong and Coleman (1994) have very appropriately named them post-divorce remarried families and post-bereavement remarried families. There are many typologies of remarried families (ibid), many factors which influence the constellation of living arrangements, and an indeterminate variety of family relationships that can develop. In this chapter, the focus is on the perceptions of remarriage among widowed persons, that is, widows and widowers in the Singaporean context. The first assumption as we embark on this subject is that widowhood is a landmark transition that has socio-emotional and economic implications for the surviving spouse. Loss of spouse through death has very different dynamics as compared to loss of spouse through divorce.

Research and literature on widowhood in the Asian context is available to some extent (Gujral, 1987; Koo, 1987; Gill and Singh, 1991; Cheng and Ma, 2000) whereas the perceptions of widows and widowers towards remarriage has received scant attention. In fact, it would not be incorrect to say that in most societies in Asia remarriage for the widowed is still a taboo subject. The reasons for this would be first, that the sanctity of marriage and the notion that marriage is for a lifetime is largely prevalent; second, that marriage is a union of not only two individuals but also two families, hence the

---

Author Note: The author would like to express her gratitude to the National University of Singapore for awarding a financial grant to conduct this research (RP 960043).

dissolution of a marriage due to death does not mean a dissolution of the alliance of the families; and third, remarriage for a young widowed person may be allowed but after middle age remarriage is considered to be inappropriate. The assumption is that once the childbearing years are past, the reason for marriage no longer exists. Conversely, if a middle-aged or older adult is known to contemplate remarriage, the relatives would speculate that his/her sexual needs are driving this desire. Due to the fear of being so misinterpreted, many widowed people shy away from even expressing such interest.

In Singapore, quantitative data on widowed persons is available from the Census (which is carried out at ten-year intervals, the latest being Year 2000), Senior Citizens surveys, 1983 and 1995, smaller studies (Singapore Council of Social Service, 1986; Lim, 1997/98; Ismail, 1997/98) and a recent study carried out by the author and Dr P. Teo (Mehta and Teo, 2000). Apart from the last mentioned research, none of the others have enquired about attitudes towards remarriage.

The Census 2000 shows that there are 118,017 widowed persons above the age of fifty years in Singapore. Of these, 19 percent are males and 81 percent females. The three main ethnic cultural groups which comprise the Singapore population, that is, Chinese, Malays, and Indians, form 79 percent, 16 percent and 6 percent of the total widowed population respectively (Singapore Department of Statistics, 2000).

The *Statistics on Marriages and Divorces 1999* has a section on grooms and brides by previous marital status, which allows a researcher to extract the number of remarriages. At this juncture, it is relevant to mention that in Singapore non-Muslims register their marriages under the Women's Charter while the Muslims marry under the Muslim Law Act. Muslims may belong to any of the ethnic groups; however, in reality the majority are Malays, followed by Indians. Very few Chinese are members of the Islamic faith. The statistics reveal that remarriage is more prevalent among the Muslims as compared to the non-Muslims (Singapore Department of Statistics, 1999). Since the focus here is on those of fifty years and above who are widowed, the rate of remarriage was calculated based upon the number who remarried divided by the number of widowed people in that category. For Muslims the rate was 0.5 percent and for the non-Muslims it was 0.1 percent. For both the non-Muslims and

Muslims, the number of widowers who remarried far exceeded the number of widows. However, the ratio was 4:1 for male and female non-Muslims while it was 2:1 for male and female Muslims.

The present paper is based on part of the findings of a larger study on widows and widowers in Singapore. While the objectives of the larger study conducted from 1997-1999 was to gather data on the health, economic, and social consequences of widowhood as well as the coping strategies applied by the sample, the present paper focuses on the results of the enquiry on their views of remarriage and the reasons given for their views.

A quantitative-cum-qualitative methodology was designed, comprising a survey of 237 widows and widowers (aged fifty years and above) and twenty-five case studies. All but two case studies consisted of respondents who were part of the survey sample. Several sources were tapped for obtaining a survey sample such as social service agencies, visitors at an exhibition on senior citizens, and through the snowballing technique. The gender and ethnic proportions of the survey sample closely followed the national sample of widowed people according to the Census of Population, 1990 (Mehta, 2001). The socio-demographic characteristics of the survey sample are shown in table 8.1.

Survey Findings

The findings on perceptions towards remarriage will be divided into findings from the survey and findings from the case studies.

Overwhelmingly, 94 percent of the survey respondents were negative about the idea of remarriage. Of the 222 who replied negatively, 60 percent were prepared to give a reason. The reasons they gave are shown in table 8.2. Eighty-nine respondents did not give reasons for their negative perception. Since it was a personal matter, their response was respected and not probed further. This is a sensitive area and it is possible that respondents did not feel comfortable discussing such matters, particularly if others were present.

Interestingly, the reasons given in table 8.2 are a mixture of societal disapproval, children's disapproval, society's age-related norms, and personal factors. As the literature informs us, the considerations for remarriage are very complex (Talbott, 1998; Poppel, 1995; Wu, 1995) and interrelated with the life stage (and age) of the widow/er, religious beliefs, and availability of prospective suitors.

Table 8.1
Selected Demographic Characteristics of Survey Sample

	Number	%
Age Distribution		
50-60	54	23
61-70	70	30
71-80	70	30
>80	43	18
Gender Distribution		
Male	46	19
Female	191	81
Ethnic Distribution		
Chinese	152	64
Malay	45	19
Indian	31	13
Other	9	4
Religious Affiliation		
Buddhist/Taoist/Ancestor Worship	107	45
Muslim	59	25
Christian	40	17
Hindu	22	9
No religion	9	4

Table 8.2
Considerations for Negative Attitude to Remarriage

	No.	%
Too old to consider remarriage	49	37
Never thought about it	34	26
Satisfied with present lifestyle	13	10
Children may not get along with 'new' parent	10	8
Financial insecurity	9	7
Not keen to make changes in life	7	5
Still faithful to late spouse	6	5
Children opposed to remarriage	2	2
Lose 'face' / society negative	1	1
No suitable suitors	1	1
Against own religion	1	1
Total	133	100
Not sure / no answer	89	
	n = 222	

Only 5 percent of the sample replied positively and 1 percent (two individuals) did not respond. The gender breakdown for the thirteen positive respondents was eight male and five female. Of the positive, four were Malay and nine were Chinese respondents. None of the Indian respondents replied positively. The positive reasons given are shown in table 8.3.

Table 8.3

Reasons for Positive Perception of Remarriage

	No.
Loneliness / need companion	5
Need someone to look after me	2
Financial reason	3
Children's encouragement	1
Leave to God / Fate	1
Not sure	1
Total	13

Perceptions towards remarriage are shaped not only by one's individual beliefs, values, and circumstances but also by society's norms and expectations. In a multicultural society like Singapore, general social norms are overshadowed by the cultural norms and particular traditions of one's ethnic community. As seen in table 8.3, the positive perceptions were backed by largely personal reasons, while one person mentioned God and the related idea of Fate as defining her positive attitude. She meant that although she was in favor of remarriage, God and fate had to be on her side for it to materialize.

Findings from Case Studies

To shed more light and depth on the survey data, the twenty-five case studies were analyzed carefully not only for the explanations but also for cross-cultural similarities and differences. Table 8.4 gives the breakdown by ethnicity and gender of the qualitative sample.

In terms of living arrangements, twenty-one out of the twenty-five subjects lived with their children; one lived with a grandchild, one with a friend, and three lived alone.

The interviewers for the case studies were matched according to ethnic culture and language of respondent to ensure a meaningful

Table 8.4
Ethnic and Gender Mix of Case Studies

	Chinese	Malay	Indian	Total
Male	4	2	1	7
Female	12	4	3	19
Total	16	6	4	25

interview. Apart from the enquiry into their feelings about remarriage, the case subjects were also asked (selectively) about their biological (sexual) needs. Bearing in mind the age group and the sensitivity of the last topic, only those respondents who seemed open to a frank discussion were selected. Hence, not all twenty-five cases were included in the discussion on sexual needs.

Overall, nineteen of the twenty-five case respondents were against the idea of remarriage. The reasons given by respondents for not being in favor ranged from personal loyalty to late spouse, being afraid of a strained marital relationship, anxious about the negative reactions of children and other relatives, afraid of choosing the wrong person, and worry that the children would be ill-treated by the 'new' parent. The quotations below illustrate some of these points:

(Sixty-nine-year-old Chinese widow who lives with her unmarried youngest daughter, and mentally handicapped eldest daughter)

> One good husband is good enough. I am also afraid that my children will look down on me. I can't do this.

(Sixty-five-year-old Chinese widow who lives with her married son and his family)

> Definitely no. I am such an old age already. People will laugh at me. If you are over 30 years old you can still think about it, but I am already over 60 years old. My grandchildren have already grown up. No need for this *(remarriage)*.

(Sixty-eight-year-old Malay widower who lived with his married son and his family)

> I am afraid that others will laugh at me and I can't afford to support her.

(Sixty-two-year-old Chinese widow who lives with her bachelor son)

> What if I find someone with lots of illness and I will need to take care of him. I won't have freedom to go out.

(Chinese widow, aged seventy-five years, who lives with her three unmarried daughters)

> I don't think about remarriage. I already have children and grandchildren. I follow the Chinese tradition teaching where a woman could not remarry after her husband dies.

(Chinese widow, aged sixty-two, who lives with her unmarried daughter)

> I read in the newspapers that remarriages often resulted in step-parents ill treating the children or having many complications. Thus, I avoided remarriage.

Some were not keen because they felt that they would like to pay more attention to their spiritual growth since old age was approaching.

(Sixty-two-year-old Malay widow who was living with her grandchild)

> What is the point of marrying again? Since we are getting old, we should focus on improving our spiritual aspect of life.

To understand the high priority given to the spiritual dimension in later life in some cultures, one has to know the "cultural scripts" to which the members of the particular culture adhere. In the Malay Muslim culture, empirical research in Singapore (Mehta, 1999a) and secondary literature have documented the importance of increasing spiritual activities such as praying five times a day, reading the Koran, and carrying out good deeds. Through prayers, Malay Muslims seek to repent past sins. Good actions are believed to add "merit" to the individual's life, and this in turn enhances his/her status in the afterlife. Malay Muslims believe in the concept of Judgment Day, which takes place post-death, when Allah pronounces judgment on the individual's soul. Similarly, within the Indian Hindu culture the significance of religion and spiritual activities in old age is underscored in the cultural script.

The three Indian Hindu widows in the case studies also said that their religion had helped them cope with their spouses' death.

There were two cases of widows who mentioned that their husbands (prior to death) had urged them to remarry when the husbands were no longer alive.

(Malay widow, aged sixty-two, whose husband died seven years ago)

> I will stay a widow all my life. That is what is in my mind and nothing else. I want to be true to him alone. He did ask me to marry again when he dies. I told him that when he

dies, I would be alone till I am old. He asked if I could (manage) to do so. I told him, if God permits (it).

This Malay female was a Muslim and in her worldview, God decided one's fate. Hence, if God helped her in her decision to remain a widow, she would be able to do so.

The general pattern was for widowers to be more interested in remarriage than widows. This is in tandem with the trends in other cultures (Wu, 1995; Koo, 1987). Some widowers were interested but felt that their mature age and lack of wealth lessened their chances of finding a marital partner. One widow mentioned that she had been keen to remarry when she was younger but since she had several children, she failed to find someone suitable. A couple of respondents were very satisfied with their single again lifestyle, hence did not wish to remarry.

Analysis of the reasons in support of remarriage indicated that companionship, financial hardship, and need for care were the three main factors. A Chinese widower, aged eighty, who shared a flat with a roommate overcame his loneliness by increasing his friendship ties with friends from his church. He called them "brothers and sisters" who were like family members. He had little financial support from his children or relatives. However, the church provided some monthly financial assistance that helped him to make ends meet. Another Indian widow who expressed her uncontrollable experiences of crying in public as she could not come to terms with the sudden death of her husband, gained solace from joining the "Sai Baba" community. The Sai Baba movement is a spiritual path for its devotees.

> The Sai Baba (community) is not a religion at all. It teaches you how to lead your life, about humanity. It helps you by getting you involved in some chanting and they direct you into certain activities such as yoga classes. ... You see, I needed people around me. These people were very friendly and kind.

One sixty-nine-year-old man said he needed someone to look after him, since he had arthritis and felt lonely. That loneliness is not directly related to living arrangements is reflected in this case because he was living with his married daughter and her family. In the Singapore context, widowed individuals placed much weight on the views of their adult children towards the issue of remarriage. The explanation for this is not simple. First, if it is a dependent widow, she may feel obliged to seek the approval of her children. Second, if it is a widow/er who is co-residing with adult children and children-in-law, it would be the courteous thing to do. Asian society is, generally speaking, collectivist, which means that Asians are influenced by their social context in their daily behavior, self-image, as well as life decisions (Tu, 1985). Hence, it is not difficult to understand why the older persons are inclined to seek approval of their immediate family before considering remarriage.

Companionship is the greater need, but they fear that their family and relatives would laugh at their behavior and connect it to sexual interests.

(Sixty-five-year-old Chinese widow who lives with her married son and his family)

> I feel that you do not respect your children by behaving this way. Maybe my thinking is a bit outdated. I am against such behavior.

(Sixty-nine-year-old Malay widower who lives with his married son and his family)

> Before making the decision, I have got to see what my children have to say. Whether they agree or disagree.

Adult children's approval for remarriage is less frequently mentioned in Western literature on the subject and may have less salience in thinking about remarriage than it does in Asia. Widows in particular referred to the loss of respect faced by adult children if the elderly parent remarried. This "cultural logic" can be easily understood if the reader is familiar with the Asian mentality, whereby children are expected to take care of their widowed parent. The remarriage may be interpreted by members in the community as a step taken because the children had failed in caregiving.

The discussion on the amount of influence adult children had on the life decisions and choices made by widows and widowers is both culture-bound as well as age-related. Remarriage for a younger widow from exactly the same culture as an older widow was acceptable, as it was presumed that she required someone to "protect" her and support her, particularly if her children were young. An older widow (presumably) would be cared for by her adult children. Her filial children, ideally speaking, would meet her physical, emotional, social, and financial needs. However, cases of childless widows and widowers do occur and they have to turn to siblings, nieces and nephews, if they exist.

Of the three ethnic groups, it was found that mainly the Malays had multiple marriages and bereavements. Hence, while most of the Chinese and Indians had only one widowhood experience to recall, the Malays sometimes had two or three sequential widowhood experiences. This is related to the Muslim belief that facilitation of protection and support for a widowed Muslim woman is considered a good deed endorsed by the *Koran*. Hence, people in the Malay community would be proactive in assisting the process of remarriage. In general, it can be deduced that relative to the Chinese and Indian cultures, remarriage is more accepted in the Malay culture. The following case studies illustrate the life experiences of a Chinese widower, a Malay widow, and an Indian widow. Some facts have been modified to retain the confidentiality of the respondents. These are illustrations and are not to be construed as typical examples.

Example 1: Mr. Tan, a Chinese Widower, Aged Eighty

Mr. Tan married at the age of thirty to a Malaysian woman, who died during childbirth. Both mother and son died, leaving Mr. Tan as a young widower. After a few years he met and began a consensual union with woman in Singapore who gave birth to two children, a son and a daughter. Following twenty years of common law marriage his partner died, leaving Mr. Tan a second-time widower. He has been widowed for more than twenty years. He is disillusioned with his children, who do not seem to have time for him. His daughter gives him a small cash allowance on an irregular basis. He is satisfied with his life and has good neighbors. He receives financial support from his church (S $300 monthly) and has good church friends. Sometimes he worries about his health and wishes that his adult children would visit him more often. Mr. Tan rents a government housing flat and shares it with a stranger, as a single senior citizen is required to have a roommate before he/she is allowed to rent it. One of his hopes is to be admitted to a Senior Citizens' Home that is affordable.

Example 2: Madam Halimah, a Malay Widow, Aged Fifty-Three

Madam Halimah's story is tragic—in a span of four years she lost her sister, husband, and mother. She recalled that at the age of twenty-seven she married a Malay Muslim man of her choice. They loved each other dearly in the span of twenty-four years of marriage. He was ill for six years before he passed away. Her routine was to work in a food stall for long hours in the daytime; return home and finish the housework as well as render care to her ailing husband and mother. She had to look after her son too. Before her mother fell ill, she would keep an eye on her son while she was at work. As she was involved in casual work, she has no financial security or insurance cover. She was thrifty and thus managed to meet her monthly expenses. The burden of the medical expenses of her husband and mother took its toll on her health. She has high blood pressure, which requires her to take regular medication. Presently, due to her poor health and unstable emotional condition, she has stopped working. Her son and siblings are contributing towards the household expenses. Her hobbies are sewing and knitting. She visits her sisters often as they are the main source of solace at this time of loneliness and unhappiness.

Example 3: Madam Devi, an Indian Widow, Aged Fifty-Three

Madam Devi had an arranged marriage at the age of twenty-eight. They had a happy and fulfilling marriage—he was the breadwinner and she was the homemaker. When she was carrying their third child, her husband passed away suddenly due to an accident at his workplace. She had a traumatic bereavement period, as she was pregnant and her children were still young. She relied on neighbors who helped out in supervising her children, while she started a full-time job. In addition, she started to get involved in a nearby Hindu temple's religious classes. Her faith and her family of origin, such as her parents and her siblings, were her pillars of support. She could discuss personal problems with her sisters, who were her confidantes. By plunging herself into her work and religious activities, she found ways to cope with her widowhood experience. Reading is her hobby so she is able to widen her horizon through the world of books. She is not in favor of the Hindu customs in relation to widows, such as wearing of white saris. In terms of status, she feels that her status has not changed after her widowhood. This is because her siblings look up to her as she is the eldest child, and her father accords her due regard. She has been looking after him ever since her mother died five years ago. Madam Devi considers her health to be good, partly as a result of her regular Yoga classes. She does voluntary work at the Hindu temple and feels her children love her very much.

Sexual Needs

As mentioned earlier, this topic was broached only to those case respondents who were assessed to be open on the subject of sexual needs. The question was worded thus: "Do you feel that you have any biological i.e. sexual needs? If yes, how are they being met?"

The three men admitted having biological urges but had found ways to handle them, without having sexual partners. One said that he masturbated when aroused, for example, when reading *Playboy*-type magazines. Another said that he used to visit prostitutes overseas in his younger days but now, as he is eighty years old, *"I don't have the strength and need for this. I am old already."*

The third said, *"I just forget about it."* He had been recently widowed, and although he was often aroused such as when watching television, he was afraid to visit brothels because of the risk of contacting sex-related diseases. He continued, *"If someone were to introduce a widow who is willing I won't mind. It's all right to have a sexual relationship but I won't think of marrying her. I'm afraid others will laugh at me, and I can't afford to support her."*

In addition to the anticipated ridicule of friends and relatives, another consideration that prevented him from remarrying was the lack of financial resources to support a wife. Indeed, in a society which does not have a welfare state ideology, and therefore no pension for the ordinary retired person, savings of a retiree may just barely be sufficient to support one person. How could he even consider the thought of supporting another individual?

The ten women had an interesting variety of views. Two women frankly stated that men, because of their biological and hormonal condition, have stronger urges than women. Hence, they were more likely to seek sexual satisfaction. *"Women belong more to the introvert side. Whatever we do, we think of the children ... such promiscuous behavior would lose their regard for us."*

Two of them said that their late husbands had been ill for more than five years prior to their death, and hence they had become accustomed to not having a sexual life. One husband had been diabetic and had been impotent for several years. *"It's like normal because it's been so long. I don't remember it any more. We women are like that."*

Two women compared Eastern cultural norms with Western ones, as they perceived them.

For example, *"For Westerners, I think, everything is sex. Men can comfort them (women) on the bed. I won't think that for Asian women. ... I feel their morals are so different."*

Three women said that their sexual desires were buried with their late husbands. No other men would be able to replace the love their late spouses had given them. The close connection between "love" and "sex" within the marital relationship, which is seen as a sacred commitment, underpins their statements. In addition, in the Asian cultures represented in this study, older generations subscribe to the idea that for a woman, marriage should be for life. Hence, even after the husband's death the bond is not viewed as severed—the two souls are still "connected." Thus, the idea of being comforted by another man even in times of bereavement was not seen as acceptable within the respondent's culture.

One of the women went on to say that she had no sexual urges because her spiritual life had instilled a discipline in her. Initially she had missed her husband's hugs, specially *"on rainy days,"* but later as she got busy with raising her children she had no more time to think about it. Another widow mentioned that she had been diabetic for many years. She had read that people with diabetes had diminished sexual urges and thought this might explain her lack of sexual interest. Finally, one of the women commented that she felt that having a social companion was acceptable but she would not consider having a sexual partner: *"I read from the newspaper that some women who are in a similar situation as me looked for sexual partners but got cheated by them, even financially. I feel that finding a companion is all right but it is not necessary to look for sexual partner."*

From the above quotation, it can be seen that widows may perceive themselves as vulnerable, particularly in the financial sense. Entering into a relationship can jeopardize a woman's status and reputation within her family and community. Emotionally she may invest in a relationship that could turn out to be a disappointment. Socially, she may find that the association with her male partner has made her the center of "gossip" among her family members and ethno-cultural community. While the Chinese community is large, the Malay and Indian communities are minority groups and "gossip" can ruin a person's reputation. Relationships with significant others could be soured with serious consequences. Financially, she may be blackmailed by the newfound partner or conned into loaning some precious savings to him. While it is also possible for widowers to be susceptible to similar circumstances outlined in this paragraph, in a conservative Asian society such as Singapore, the chances are much lower.

On the whole, one wonders if men acknowledge their sexual desires and find ways to deal with them, and women are socialized not to acknowledge and therefore assume they do not have such desires? Or, is it true that women's sexual urges diminish after they reach menopause? The author is of the opinion that more research is needed to tease out the biological and cultural aspects of sexuality. While there is sufficient evidence to support the idea that sexual needs have a place in the lives of widows and widowers, the response to these needs is shaped by cultural beliefs and societal expectations. These beliefs and expectations change over time as well, in tandem with other social changes. In some societies it is acceptable to manage sexual needs by arrangements such as 'living apart together'—an arrangement that allows space to each partner while meeting their need for intimacy. However, in societies where most older widows and widowers are living within the family fold, such an arrangement is unlikely to arise, especially if adult children disapprove.

A Chinese widower made an interesting observation. He said that he found Taiwanese widows more likely to respond to his friendly advances as compared to Singaporean widows. He observed that the latter were too preoccupied with grandchildren and household duties!

In the sample of twenty-five case studies, there were two cases, a widow aged fifty-three and a widower aged sixty-eight, who were still caring for their elderly parents who had crossed eighty years. Caring for them was also part of their family duty. The ladder of filial exchanges within the family was in these cases both a matter of "giving" and "receiving." With the global ageing of populations, four-generational families are becoming more prevalent. This increases the number of senior citizens receiving and giving filial care (for more details on the intergenerational exchanges of care between generations, see Mehta, 1999b).

It is to be noted that widows often immersed themselves in family responsibilities and this distracted them from their personal needs. Over time, this may become their "normal" lifestyle. Both widows and widowers seemed to fear the ridicule of society if they remarried. This may change over time with newer cohorts of elderly who may have different views of social behavior in later life. Hence, it should be noted that these findings are limited to the current cohorts of widows and widowers. With greater exposure to other cultures, the television and other media, increased traveling and educational opportunities, future cohorts of widows and widowers may have less traditional views of remarriage. They may also be less restricted by societal disapproval.

The term "sunset love" or "autumn love" is often used in Singapore to describe the phenomenon of two older adults involved in an intimate relationship after divorce or widowhood (Hall, 1997: 101). To date, the subject is rarely discussed or acknowledged as a real option for widows and widowers in Singapore. However, there are signs that it is beginning to spark some lively debate. The Singapore Action Group of Elders (SAGE) have had two workshops on "Autumn Love" in English and Mandarin, and the feedback was very positive. The "young old" are beginning to question societal values and mores regarding the topic of intimacy in later years.

Conclusion

The paper has examined the Singaporean perceptions of remarriage from a study of 237 widows and widowers, including twenty-five case studies. The interdependent nature of the Asian psyche (Markus and Kitayama, 1991), as well as the cultural norms surrounding the idea of "a marriage is for a lifetime" and "spousal loyalty," prevail with respect to perceptions of remarriage. However, of the three ethnic groups, the Malay culture seems to accept the idea of remarriage more than the Chinese and Indian cultures. The former is perhaps linked to the emphasis in the *Koran* on protection of women, including widows by men in the community through remarriage. Across the three communities, there existed greater acceptance of remarriage by widowers as compared to widows. On the other hand, widows tend to be embedded in the immediate family cocoon in Singapore and may prefer that security as opposed to the uncertainty of a second marriage.

This study has implications for research and policy as elaborated elsewhere (Teo and Mehta, 2001). The findings are restricted in their generality due to the small sample size and lack of representativeness. However, the researchers have tried to ensure variability in the survey sample and case studies to illustrate the typical situations and challenges faced by widowed persons in Singapore. The research findings fill a gap in the data on this target population and their views on remarriage and their personal needs. There are implications for public education on ageing and societal acceptance of the need for companionship among widowed people. When their suggestions were invited, some remarked that voluntary groups could be established for greater interaction among widows and widowers so that their social lives could be of better quality.

References

Cheng, B. Y., and Ma, L. C. (2000). Stress, social support and quality of life of bereaved spouses in Hong Kong, *Asia Pacific Journal of Social Work*, 10 (1), 37-59.

Ganong, L. H., and Coleman, M. (1994). *Remarried family relationships*. London: Sage.

Gill, S., and Singh, M. P. (1991). Widowhood: Perceptions and coping strategies. *Indian Journal of Behaviour*, 15 (1), 14-19.

Gujral, J. S. (1987). Widowhood in India. In H. Z. Lopata (Ed.), *Widows: Vol. 1 The Middle East, Asia and the Pacific*. Durham: Duke University Press.

Hall, C. (1997). *Daughters of the dragon: Women's lives in contemporary China*. London: Scarlet Press.

Ismail, Raihan Bte (1996/97). *Social support of elderly Malay widows*. Department of Social Work and Psychology, National University of Singapore. Unpublished Honours Thesis.

Koo, J. (1987). Widows in Seoul, Korea. In H. Z Lopata. (Ed.), *Widows: Vol. 1 The Middle East, Asia and the Pacific*. Durham: Duke University Press.

Lim, H. T. (1997/98). *Close friendships among Chinese widowed elderly*. Department of Social Work and Psychology, National University of Singapore. Unpublished Honours Thesis.

Markus, H. R., and Kitayama, S. (1991). Culture and the self: Implications for cognition, emotion and motivation. *Psychological Review*, 98 (2), 224-253.

Mehta, K. (1999a). Ethnic integrative patterns of Singaporean very old persons. *Generations Review*, 9 (2), 4-5.

Mehta, K. (1999b). Intergenerational Exchanges: Qualitative Evidence from Singapore. *Southeast Asian Journal of Social Science*, 27 (2), 111-122.

Mehta, K. (2001). Widowhood in Singapore. *Awareness: Journal of the Association for Action and Research*, 8, 41-55.

Mehta, K., and Teo, P. (2000). *Voices of the heart: Widows and widowers in Singapore*. Singapore: Humanities Press.

O'Bryant, S. L., and Hansson, R. (1995). Widowhood. In R. O. Blieszner and V. H. Bedford. (Eds.), *Handbook of aging and the family* (pp. 440-458). Westport, CT: Greenwood Press.

Poppel, F. V. (1995). Widows, widowers, and remarriage in Nineteenth Century Netherlands. *Population Studies*, 49, 421-441.

Singapore Council of Social Service. (1986). *Report on a study of widowed families*. Singapore: Singapore Council of Social Service.

Singapore Department of Statistics. (1999). *Statistics on marriages and divorces 1999*. Singapore: Department of Statistics.

Singapore Department of Statistics. (2000). *Census of population, Singapore: Advance data release*. Singapore: Department of Statistics.

Talbott, M. M. (1998). Older widows' attitudes towards men and remarriage. *Journal of Aging Studies*, 12 (4), 429-449.

Teo, P., and Mehta, K. (2001). Participating in the home: Widows cope in Singapore. *Journal of Aging Studies,* 5 (2),127-144.

Tu, W. M. (1985). Selfhood and otherness in Confucian thought. In A. J. Marsella, G. Davos and F. L. K. Tsu (Eds.), *Culture and self: Asian and western perspectives.* New York: Tavistock.

Wu, Z. (1995). Remarriage after widowhood: A marital history study of older Canadians. *Canadian Journal on Aging,* 14 (4), 719-736.

Contributors

Kate Davidson is lecturer in the Department of Sociology, University of Surrey, UK. She is co-director of the Centre for Research on Ageing and Gender and her research interests include the health behaviors and social networks of older men.

Graham Fennell is professor of sociology and social policy at Roehampton University of Surrey in the UK and European editor of *Ageing International*. His book *The Sociology of Old Age* (with C. Phillipson and H. Evers) (Open University Press) has been widely used. His current interests include sexuality, and the sociology of everyday life. In 2002 his translation with a new Introduction of Hans Zetterberg's *Sexual Life in Sweden* was published by Transaction Publishers.

Klas Borell is professor of sociology in the Department of Social Work, Mid-Sweden University in Östersund, Sweden. He is presently engaged in a research project on ageing and the meaning of home.

Deborah Carr is assistant professor in the Department of Sociology and the Institute for Health, Health Care, and Aging Policy at Rutgers University in New Brunswick, NJ, USA. Her current research interests include health and well-being over the life course, late-life bereavement, and end-of-life planning and decision making.

Jenny de Jong Gierveld is honorary fellow at the Netherlands Interdisciplinary Demographic Institute (NIDI) and professor in the Department of Sociology and Social Gerontology at the Vrije Universiteit Amsterdam, the Netherlands.

Sophie Ghazanfareeon Karlsson is a doctoral candidate in Social Work the Department of Social Work, Mid-Sweden University, Östersund, Sweden. Her dissertation focuses on LAT relationships of older people in Sweden.

Kalyani K. Mehta is associate professor in the Department of Social Work and Psychology, National University of Singapore. Her research interests include social policies affecting older people, cross-cultural patterns of ageing, dynamics of caregiving for older kin, and grandparenting.

Alinde J. Moore is professor and chair of the Department of Psychology, Ashland University, Ashland, Ohio, USA. Her research interests include ageing, coping strategies, widowhood, and qualitative research methods.

Nan Stevens is associate professor in the Department of Psychogerontology at the University of Nijmegen and professor of Applied Gerontology in the Department of Social Gerontology at the Free University in Amsterdam, the Netherlands. Her research focuses on factors contributing to well-being in later life, widowhood, friendship and new partner relationships.

Dorothy C. Stratton is professor of social work and chair of the Department of Social Work at Ashland University in Ashland, Ohio, USA. Her research interests are men's issues, social relationships and ageing, widowhood, and qualitative methodologies.

Rebecca Utz is a doctoral candidate in the Department of Sociology at the University of Michigan. In Fall 2004, she will be assistant professor of sociology at University of Utah in Salt Lake City, UT. Her research interests include ageing and the life course, health, and the social causes and consequences of obesity.

Deborah Kestin van den Hoonaard is associate professor in the Department of Gerontology at St Thomas University in New Brunswick, Canada. Her research interests include ageing and gender, widowhood, and qualitative research methods.

Index

ageing: Priestly on, vii–viii; sexual activity and, viii; "young old," 1
Allan, G., 123
America. *See* United States
anger: widowhood, 29, 37
Antonucci, T. C., 123
anxiety: post-loss anxiety, 29, 34; "special event" grief, 36, 37
Arber, S., 71
Ariza, M., 79
Asia: collectivism, 151; marriage, 143–144, 155; remarriage, 143–144, 150–151; sexual activity, xii
autonomy: cohabitation, 9; LAT relationships, 6–9, 15, 96–97; marriage, 9; repartnering, 60, 61–62, 96–97; in United States, 41; widowers, 127; widows, 15, 50, 108; women, 15
"autumn love," 157

Becker, G., 13, 14
Berardo, F. M., 122, 131
Bereavement Index, 24
birthdays: depression on, 37
Borell, K., 80, 130
Bulcroft, K. A., 128–129, 130
Bulcroft, R. A., 128–129, 130
Burch, T. K., 134

Caine, Lynn, *Widow,* 109
Canada: "current woman" in, 118; remarriage rate for widowers, 134; widowers in, 106; widows in, 106. *See also* New Brunswick (Canada)
Carr, D., 28
"Casserole Brigade," 116–117, 136–137
Caughlin, J. P., 13
Changing Lives of Older Couples (CLOC) study, 22–41; adjustment to late-life spousal loss, 20, 32–35; "anniversary" grief, 36–37; cohorts, 40; death expectedness, 26–29; death quality and survivor adjustment, 28–29, 39; dyadic characteristics of spousal death, 20, 25, 39; individual-level attributes and spousal loss, 20, 25, 31, 39–40; late-life longevity, 20, 25-30; macrosocial condition of spousal loss, 20, 25, 39; marital quality and spousal grief, 20, 30–32, 39; NEO Five-Factor Personality Inventory, 31-32; research topics, 20; "special event" grief, 20, 36–38; strengths, 23–24; survey sample, 22–23
children: acceptance of parent's LAT partner, 100; Asian, 150–151; remarriage by parent, 114, 146t2, 147t3, 150–151; support for parents, xii, 34, 40, 150–151; support from parents, xii, 34–35
Chinese culture: remarriage, xiv, 144, 152
Christianity: sex-negativity, ix
cohabitation (unmarried): age at start, 90, 91, 93; age difference between partners, 88; autonomy, 9; difficulty tracking, 47; divorce (prior), 91, 93; educational level, 91, 93; Europe, xiv; financial considerations, 97–98; framework, 67; LAT relationships, 2, 3; living arrangements, 99; loneliness, 49, 92, 94–95; motives for choosing, 94–95; *särbo* and, 4; *särboende* and, 5; studies of, 87; Sweden, 2, 4; time since former relationship, 90–91, 93
Coleman, M., 143
companionship arrangements, 125
consummate partnerships, 52–56; characteristics, 53, 59; earlier marriages compared to, 55; functions served by, 58; LAT relationships compared to, 53; loneliness, 56; prevalence, 60, 62; sexual activity, 53; ties to the deceased, 54–55

163

Crohan, S. E., 123
"current woman," 121–142; activity-based friendship, 128; in Canada, 118; *companion* vs. *partner,* 126–127; companionship arrangements, 125; definition, 118, 121–122; female companions, 125; interaction based on practical help, 127; negotiations with, 135–138; partner relationship with sexual activity, 129–131; partner relationship without sexual activity, 128–129; relationship patterns, 126–127; relatives as, 125, 139; sexual activity, 124; in United States, 118; wives, 125

Davidson, K., 133
De Oliveira, O., 79
death. *See* spousal death
depression: "anniversary" grief, 36–37; birthdays, 37; widowhood, 20–22, 31
divorce: after fifty, 85; cohorts, 40; remarriage rate, 68–69; repartnering, 91, 93; Sweden, 2; United States, 35; women, 16
Dixon, R., 67, 81
Doyle, V., 117
Dutch Aging Survey (DAS), 51–62
"dying well," 28–29
Dykstra, P., 49

Erikson, E. H., 132
Europe: remarriage, xiv; repartnering, xiv; sex-negativity, ix. *See also* Great Britain; Sweden; United Kingdom

faithfulness: LAT relationships, 7
family life: binuclear families, 2; caretaker role, xii; changing patterns, 1–2; families of choice, 2; households and, 2; immediate family cocoon, 126, 157; nuclear families, 19; older couples, 6; recombinant families, 2; restructuring of, 15–16
Ferraro, K. F., 123
freedom: to widows, widowers, 117
friendships: activity-based friendship, 128; cross-sex friendships, 128; men, 123, 128; older people, 123, 128; United States, 28; widowers, 71, 123; widowhood, 123, 128; widows, 50, 71, 110–113, 123; women, 123

Ganong, L., 86, 143
Gass, K. A., 127
gender: in bereavement research, 39-40
gender revolution: Sweden, 16
Giddens, A., 88
Gierveld, J. D., 135, 136
Ginn, J., 71
Glaser, B. G., 124
"good death," 28–29
gossip: repartnering, 112–113, 114, 155; Singapore, 155
Great Britain: remarriage, 48. *See also* United Kingdom
grief: "anniversary" grief, 36–37; attributes of the deceased, 20, 31–32; denial of, 32; marital quality and spousal grief, 20, 30–32, 39; normative expectations for expression, 32, 71, 119n8; scales, 24; "special event" grief, 20, 36–38; troubled marriages, 30; widowhood, 22
Grimes, J., 123
Grinwald, S., 138

Hagestad, G. O., 123
Hatch, R. G., 67, 81
Haven, C., 123
health: LAT relationships, 5, 11, 70; older people, 6; repartnering, xiii, 6, 70, 139
healthcare: in Sweden, 11, 13
Henry, C. S., 101
Hollander, J., 77
"homemaker's investment," 77–78
Hospice movement, 28
households: division of household labor, 16, 108; maintaining a household after spousal death, 33–35; multi-household constellations, 2; one-person households, 85, 101
Howard, J., 77
"husband sanctification," 107

immediate family cocoon: widowers, 126; widows, 157
Indian culture: remarriage, xiv, 149
individualism: United States, 41
International Association of Gerontology (IAG), 17th Congress, x–xi
intimacy/intimate relationships: changing patterns, 1–2; LAT relationships, 6–7, 15; marital intimacy, 133; widowers, 15, 124–125

Johnson, C. L., 123
Johnson, M. E., 13
Johnson, M. P., 13

Karlsson, S., 80, 130

LAT relationships (Living Apart Together), 1–18, 65–83; acceptance by children, 100; activeness of partners, 5; age at start, 90, 91, 93; age difference between partners, 88, 90; autonomy, 6–9, 15, 96–97; "best of both worlds," xiv; caring for partner, 11–13, 16, 75–76, 82, 101; choice of separate households, 6; cohabitation (unmarried), 2, 3; consummate partnerships compared to, 53; continuity of life as usual, 100; definition, 13, 102n1; distance between domiciles, 6; division of labor, 9–10, 12, 15; divorce (prior), 91, 93; driving force behind, 7; duration of relationship, 6, 10–11; educational level, 91, 93; emotional support, 11, 15, 16–17; Europe, xiv; faithfulness, 7; financial considerations, 10–11, 97–98; future care, 11–13; gender revolution, 16; health of partners, 5, 11, 70; institutionalization of, 4, 14; intimacy in, 6–7, 15; joint resources, 10–11, 14; living arrangements, 99–100, 156; loneliness, 49, 92, 94; marriage compared to, 13–14; meeting place, 80; moral commitment, 15; motives for choosing, 7–9, 12–13, 15–16, 94, 96–97, 101; New Brunswick (Canada), 112; official statistics, 4; ownership of resources, 14; popularity, 3; remarriage, 92; *särbo*, 4; *särboende*, 5; sexual activity, 79; significance, 92; stressfulness of repartnering, 101; structural foundations, 14; studies of, 2–3, 13, 87; survey sample, 4–6, 66–67; Sweden, 1–18; time since former relationship, 90–91, 93; time spent together, 6; United Kingdom, 65–83; wealth of partners, 5, 70; widows, 90; "young old" in, 3
Levin, I., 79
Levine, I., 130
Lewis, B., ix

living alone: loneliness, 92, 99, 100; to widows, widowers, 117
loneliness: cohabitation, 49; cohabitation (unmarried), 92, 94–95; consummate partnerships, 56; de Jong Gierveld scale (Dutch scale), 51, 92; desire for a new partner, 52; LAT relationships, 49, 92, 94; living alone, 92, 99, 100; remarriage, 49, 92, 147t3; repartnering, xii, 60, 72, 85, 92, 94–95, 100; steady companions, 58; widowers, 73, 125; widowhood, xii, 33, 49–50, 72
longevity, 20, 25–30
Lopata, H. Z., 49, 66, 107, 134
Lovelace, S. G., 101
Lowenthal, M., 123
Lund, D. A., 127

Malay culture: remarriage, xiv, 149, 152, 155
marriage: age at, 67; age difference between partners, 131; Asia, 143–144, 155; autonomy, 9; availability of partners, 67; childbearing, 144; commuter marriages, 2; companionate love, 61; consummate partnerships compared to earlier marriages, 55; division of household labor, 16, 108; Dixon's framework, 67–68; feasibility of, 67; freedom contrasted to, 117; gendered duties, 9, 34–36; "homemaker's investment," 77–78; "husband sanctification," 107; LAT relationships compared to, 13–14; marital intimacy, 133; marital quality and spousal grief, 20, 30–32, 39; marital-specific capital, 14; "marriage capital," 77; proportion never marrying, 67; sexual activity, 129; Sweden, 4; United States, 34; unsatisfactory experiences, xi
Mehta, K. K., 126
men: coming home, 58, 74; emotional needs, 49–50; friendships, 123, 128; heterosexual relationships, 49–50; life expectancy, 86–87; marital status at death, 87; remarriage, 90. *See also* older men; widowers
Moore, H. J., 118
Moss, M. S., 47, 49, 75, 138
Moss, S., 47, 49, 75, 138

National Death Index (NDI), 23
NEO Five-Factor Personality Inventory, 31–32
NESTOR-Living Arrangements and Social Networks (LSN) study, 89–102
Netherlands: repartnering, 51–62, 89–102; state pension, 97–98, 102n2; survey sample, 51, 89–90
New Brunswick (Canada): demographics, 106–107; LAT relationships, 112; repartnering, 105–119; survey sample, 105–106
new partners. *See* repartnering
nursing home patients: death of, 30; preparation for widowhood, 30

older men: companionship arrangements, 125; family relationships, 126; importance of sex, 131–133; remarriage considerations, 49; remarriage rate, 133; studies of, 122; United States, 122. *See also* widowers
Older Men's Lives (Thompson), 122
older people: cross-sex friendships, 128; dating scene, 136; filial care, 156; friendships, 123; health, 6; living arrangements of, 86; one-person households, 85, 101; sex ratio, 35, 69, 122; sexual activity, ix; social integration, 86
older women: "Casserole Brigade," 116–117, 136–137; nontraditional partnerships, 49; remarriage considerations, 3; remarriage rate, 133; studies of, 122; United States, 122. *See also* widows

Parkes, C. M., xii
Patient Self-Determination Act (1990), 28
Present Feelings About Loss, 24
Preston, D., 123
Priestly, J. B.: on ageing, vii–viii
Pyke, K. D., 100–101

religion: remarriage, 95–96, 146t2, 147t3; repartnering, 95–96; sexual activity, 129–130; spousal death, 41, 149
remarriage: age and acceptability of, 144, 146t2, 151; age at start, 90, 91, 92, 93; age difference between partners, 131; Asia, xiv, 143–144, 150–151; availability of partners, 68–69, 107; childbearing, 144; children's attitudes, 114, 146t2, 147t3, 150–151; Chinese culture, xiv, 144, 152; cohorts, 41; comparing one's wives, 138–139; considerations, 72–78, 87–88, 107–117, 133–134, 145; cultural approval, 99; desire for a new partner, 71–72, 150; divorce (prior), 91, 93; educational level, 91, 93; Europe, xiv; feasibility of, 70–71; financial considerations, 97–98, 130, 146t2, 147t3, 154, 155–156; finding a new spouse, 134–135; Great Britain, 48; "homemaker's investment," 77–78; horror stories, 110; Indian culture, xiv, 149; LAT relationships, 92; loneliness, 49, 92, 147t3; Malay culture, xiv, 152, 155; marital history, 69, 132–133; meaningfulness, 47; men, 90; motives for choosing, 94–96, 99; Muslim *vs.* non-Muslim populations in Singapore, 144–145; older men, 49; older women and, 3; opportunity for, x, 50, 66, 87, 137; perceptions of, 147; post-divorce *vs.* post-bereavement, 143; promise not to remarry, 108; promise to remarry, 149–150; rate of, 48, 68–69, 86, 90, 92–94, 105, 133, 144–145; reasons against, 47, 74–78, 100, 107–108, 110, 145–147, 148–149; reasons for, 147, 150–151; religious values, 95–96, 146t2, 147t3; ridicule for, 156–157; sex ratio of older people, 69; someone already known, 134–135; studies of, 65–66, 87; survey sample, 145, 146t1, 147–148; ties to/yearning for deceased spouse, 138; time since former relationship, 90–91, 93; United States, 48, 86; wealth, 102; Western world, 3; widowers' attitudes toward, 115–117, 133–134; widows' attitudes toward, 107–115; women, 50, 90
repartnering: age at start, 90, 91, 92, 93; age difference between partners, viii–ix, 60, 88, 90, 131; autonomy, 60, 61–62, 96–97; availability of partners, 67, 68–69, 107; awareness of alternatives to remarriage, 62; barriers to, 110–113; cohort behavior, 32, 35, 41, 92,

156–157; considerations, 72–78, 87–88, 107–118, 133–134, 145; consummate partnerships, 52–56, 58, 59, 60, 62; continuity in lifestyles, 60; control of the relationship, 116–117; current quality of life, xii; dating scene, 136; desire for a new partner, 48, 52, 60, 67, 71–72, 79, 81, 82, 115–116, 123–124, 132–133; divorce (prior), 91, 93; Dixon's framework, 67–68; educational level, 91, 93–94; Europe, xiv; expectations, 135–136; failed partnerships, 59; feasibility of, 67, 70–71; financial considerations, 10–11, 97–98, 99, 102; first three years of widowhood, 62; former relationships, xi; "gold digging," xiv; gossip, 112–113, 114, 155; health, xiii, 6, 70, 139; internal dialogue prior to, 61; issues needing resolution, 61; life-strategies, 88; living arrangements, 91; loneliness, xii, 33, 60, 72, 85, 92, 94–95, 100; motives for choosing, 7–9, 12–13, 15–16, 60, 94–98, 101; Netherlands, 51–62, 89–102; New Brunswick (Canada), 105–119; opportunity for, 50, 87, 98–99; paradoxical attitudes, 118; partner relationship with sexual activity, 129–131; partner relationship without sexual activity, 128–129; patterns of, 87; pensions, 97–98, 99, 130; post-divorce vs. post-bereavement, 143; potential disadvantages, 61; rate of, 90; religious values, 95–96; service provider relationships, 58–59; social isolation, 85, 122; steady companions, 56–58, 59, 60; stressfulness, 101; survey sample, 51, 89–90, 105–106; time since former relationship, 90–91, 93, 94, 139; wealth, xiii–xiv, 5, 70, 102; wedding rings, 108–110, 114, 118, 118n3; widows compared to widowers, 48, 118. See also cohabitation (unmarried); LAT relationships (Living Apart Together); remarriage
Roberts, G., 79
Rubenstein, R. L., 130

särbo, 4
särboende, 5
Seidler, V. J., 128

sexual activity: age difference between partners, viii–ix, 131; ageing and, viii; "approved" relationships, x, xi, 71; Asia, xii; as a benefit, xiii; cessation, vii; consummate partnerships, 53; as a cost, xiii; cultural influences, ix–x; culture lag, ix; "current woman," 124; Europe, ix; gender-related differences, ix–x; heath, 132; heterosexual relationships, 49–50; importance to older men, 131–133; LAT relationships (Living Apart Together), 79; life-enhancing aspects, x; marriage, 129; masturbation, 154; procreation, xii; prostitution, 154; religion, 129–130; repartnering with sexual activity, 129–131; repartnering without sexual activity, 128–129; sex-negativity, ix; steady companions, 56; widowers, xiii, 156; widowhood and, vii–ix, 156; widows, xiii, 111, 156; young Europeans, ix
Shabat, T., 138
Sinclair, S., 79
Singapore, 143–159; attitudes toward remarriage, xiv; "autumn love," 157; Chinese, 144, 152; cohort behavior, 156–157; gossip, 155; immediate family cocoon, 157; Indians, 144, 149; Malays, 144, 149, 152, 155; Muslim population, 144–145, 152, 157; non-Muslim population, 144–145; rate of remarriage, 144–145; sexual activity, xii; *Statistics on Marriages and Divorces 1999*, 144; "sunset love," 157; survey sample, 145, 146t1, 147–148; widowed people in, 144; "young old," 157
social isolation: repartnering, 85, 122; widowers, 122–123
spousal death: causes, 25; death expectedness, 26–28; death quality and survivor adjustment, 28–30, 39; death-related stressors, 31; depression, 20–21, 30; "dying well," 28–29; dysphoria, 21; "good death," 28–29; marital status at, 87; nursing home patients, 30; pain prior to, 29, 39; psychological distress, 20–21; religious values, 41, 149
Sternberg, R. J., 61
Stevens, N., 123

Stratton, D. C., 118
Strauss, A. L., 124
"sunset love," 157
Swain, S. O., 123, 128, 135–136
Sweden, 1–18; age difference between sexual partners, viii–ix; cohabitation, 2, 4; divorce, 2; family forms, 1–2; gender revolution, 16; healthcare system, 11, 13; LAT relationships, 1–18; marriage, 4; *särbo,* 4; *särboende,* 5; survey sample, viii–ix, 4–6

Talbott, M. M., 132
Teo, P., 144
Texas Revised Inventory of Grief, 24
Thompson, E. H., *Older Men's Lives,* 122
Troll, L. E., 123
Trost, J., 79, 130

United Kingdom: LAT relationships, 65–83; survey sample, 66–67; widows and widowers in, 66. See also Great Britain
United States, 19–46; autonomy in, 41; cause of death, 25; "current woman" in, 118; divorce, 36; friendship in, 28; gender-based social roles, 35–36; Hospice movement, 28; individualism in, 41; life expectancy, 25–26; maintaining a household after spousal death, 33–35; marriage in, 35; nuclear families, 19; older men, 122; older women, 122; Patient Self-Determination Act (1990), 28; remarriage, 48, 86; sex-negativity, ix; sex ratio of older people, 35, 122; terminology for long-term relationships not involving cohabitation, 3; widowhood, 19–46; Women's Movement (1960s), 40
Utz, R. L., 33

van den Hoonaard, D. K., 127, 134
Vinick, B. H., 122–123, 129
vulnerability: widowhood and, xii

wealth: LAT relationships, 5, 70; remarriage, 102; repartnering, xiii–xiv, 5, 70, 102
wedding rings, 108–110, 114, 118, 118n3
Widow (Caine), 109

widowers, 121–142; autonomy, 127; Canada, 106; "Casserole Brigade," 116–117, 136–137; childless, 125; coming home, 58, 74; comparing one's wives, 138–139; control of repartnering relationship, 116–117; desire for a partner, 48, 52, 60, 79, 81, 82, 115–116, 123–124, 132–133, 150; experience of spousal death, 28; freedom to, 117; friendships, 71, 123; gender-based social roles, 35–36; health, xiii, 70, 139; housework, 40; immediate family cocoon, 126; intimacy, 15, 124–125; introverted men, 126; in LAT relationships, 7–9; life expectancy, 86–87; living alone to, 117; loneliness, 73, 125; "marriage capital," 77; masturbation, 154; need for companionship, xii; prostitution, 154; remarriage considerations, 72–78, 87–88, 115–117, 133–134; remarriage opportunity, x, 66, 87, 137; remarriage rate, 48, 68–69, 92–94, 105, 134; sexual activity, xiii, 156; Singapore, 144; social isolation, 122–123; "society of widowers," 122; sons, 125; studies of, 121, 124; support for children, 34–35; support from children, xii, 34–35, 40; survey sample, 124; ties to/yearning for deceased spouse, 78, 116, 129, 132; United Kingdom, 66; wealth, xiii–xiv, 70; "widower" as an identity, 115; widowhood rate, 48; widows compared to, 48, 118; yearning for spouse, 39. See also "current woman"; older men
widowhood, 19–46; adjustment to late-life spousal loss, 20, 32–35; age and acceptability of remarriage, 144; anger, 29, 30, 37; beginning, 27; cohorts and, 32, 35, 40, 92, 156–157; cultural context, 41–42; death expectedness, 25–29; death quality and survivor adjustment, 29, 39; death-related stressors, 31; depression, 20–22, 30, 37–38; dyadic characteristics, 20, 25, 39; dysphoria following, 21; emotional support, 123; first three years, 62; friendships, 123, 128; gender-based social roles, 19, 35–36; grief, 22; individual-level at-

tributes and spousal loss, 20, 25, 31, 40; intrusive thoughts, 27; late-life (*see* Changing Lives of Older Couples (CLOC) study); late-life longevity, 25–30; loneliness, xii, 33, 49–50, 72; macrosocial conditions, 20, 25, 39; mourning period, 71; multifaceted nature, 38; normative expectations for expression of grief, 32, 71, 119n8; nursing homes as preparation for, 30; period following spousal death, 62, 71, 87–88; post-loss anxiety, 29, 34; psychological distress, 20–22; rates of, 48; remarriage opportunity, x, 66, 87, 137; repartnering, 62; sadness following, 21; self-efficacy beliefs, 41; sequential experiences, 152; sexual activity and, vii–ix; social participation, 22, 32–33; spiritual beliefs, 41; studies of, xi; support for children, xii, 34–35; support from children, xii, 34–35, 40, 150–151; ties to/yearning for deceased spouse, 29, 31, 37, 39, 48–49, 54–55, 75, 78, 107–108, 116, 129, 132, 138, 146t2; transition to, 22, 31, 85; United States, 19–46; vulnerability and, xii

widows: age and acceptability of remarriage, 151; autonomy, 15, 50, 108; Canada, 106; desire for a partner, 48, 52, 60, 79, 81, 82, 115, 150; experience of spousal death, 27; family caretaker role, xii; freedom to, 117; friendships, 50, 71, 110–113, 123; gender-based social roles, 35–36; going out from home, 58, 74; health, xiii, 70; "homemaker's investment," 77–78; housework, 40; hugs, 111; "husband sanctification," 107; immediate family cocoon, 157; LAT relationships, 90; in LAT relationships, 7–9; life expectancy, 86–87; living alone to, 117; Muslims, 152, 157; own household, 15–16; promise not to remarry, 108; promise to remarry, 149–150; relationships with men, 110–113; remarriage considerations, 72–78, 87–88, 107–115; remarriage opportunity, x, 66, 87, 137; remarriage rate, 48, 68–69, 92–94, 105; self-confidence, 101; self-sufficiency, 101; selfishness, 78; sexual activity, xiii, 111, 156; Singapore, 144; "society of widows," 66, 122; support for children, xii, 34–35; support from children, xii, 34–35, 40, 150–151; ties to/yearning for deceased spouse, 78, 107–108; United Kingdom, 66; wealth, xiii–xiv, 70; wedding rings, 108–110, 114, 118, 118n3; "widow" as an identity, 115; widowers compared to, 48, 118; widowhood rate, 48; yearning for spouse, 39. *See also* older women

women: autonomy, 15; divorce, 16; emotional needs, 49–50; friendships, 123; gender revolution, 16, 40; going out from home, 58, 74; heterosexual relationships, 49–50; life expectancy, 86–87; marital status at death, 87; paid work, 16; relationships with men, 110–113; remarriage, 50, 90; restructuring of family life, 15–16. *See also* older women; widows

Wright, P. H., 123

"young old": definition, 1; LAT relationships, 3; Singapore, 157

Zetterberg, H. L., viii, x

For Product Safety Concerns and Information please contact our EU
representative GPSR@taylorandfrancis.com
Taylor & Francis Verlag GmbH, Kaufingerstraße 24, 80331 München, Germany

www.ingramcontent.com/pod-product-compliance
Lightning Source LLC
Chambersburg PA
CBHW061836300426
44115CB00013B/2410